Endpapers Haymakers work in the
sun in County Donegal.

Right Children play
outside a Georgian doorway in Dublin.

Published by
CHARTWELL BOOKS, INC.
A Division of **BOOK SALES, INC.**
110 Enterprise Avenue
Secaucus, New Jersey 07094

This book was devised and produced by
Multimedia Publications (UK) Ltd

Editor: Marilyn Inglis
Assistant Editor: Sydney Francis
Production: Arnon Orbach
Design: John Strange and Associates
Picture Research: Sheila Corr

First published in the United States of
America 1985 by Chartwell Books, Inc.

ISBN 0-89009-835-2

Origination by D S Colour International Ltd.,
London
Printed in Italy by Poligrafici Calderara S.p.A. Bologna

IRELAND
Past and Present

Edited by Brendan Kennelly

CHARTWELL
BOOKS, INC.

Contents

Dry-stone walls built between fields in County Kerry.

Foreword

Ignorance of Ireland, both abroad and at home, declares a need for a book about the country as it is seldom seen. Although this ignorance is sometimes dispelled by Ireland's champions abroad, the need for a book written by the Irish about themselves is apparent.

This book, written by a collection of Irish authors, meets that need; Ireland is revealed as a land of beauty, of contrasts, her people bound together by a long, complex and troubled history from neolithic times to the present day.

The main cultural influence on Ireland came from the Celts, a race of tribal peoples who lived life to the full, ate and drank, feasted and loved to excess. They preferred to die in a momentary blaze of glory in battle rather than live to a ripe old age in mediocrity. The Celts, or Gaels (whose common language was Gaelic), became the dominant race in Ireland. Their rich imagination and love of stories produced the bulk of Irish myths and legends, which were passed down orally from generation to generation, until preserved in writing in the monasteries on beautifully illuminated manuscripts. The Celtic traits – love of life, words and music – are still prevalent in the Ireland of today.

A major force in Ireland is religion. What a decisive part religion has played in Ireland's turbulent history! And not only in moral issues. Most profoundly at the time of the Reformation, when Ireland and her powerful neighbor, England, went their different ways, Ireland kept faith with tradition. And again, later, when Partition took place and the nine historic counties of Ulster were truncated to a manipulatory six.

In the south, within living memory every aspect of life was denominational, even social relations. There were not only Catholic and Protestant churches, colleges and hospitals, but even banks, newspapers, social and sports clubs, shops and business houses. In Chapter 4 Terence Brown recalls that meeting in 1965, so full of hope, between Sean Lemass and Terence O'Neill, leaders of the two chunks of Ireland. They were endeavoring to establish some form of communication between the two Irelands, but fierce bigotry in Northern Ireland shattered that hope, and blasted not only O'Neill's political career, but also those of his more civilized successors.

The Republic took a decisive step towards real economic independence when it joined the European Economic Community (EEC). It was unfortunate, however, that this took place at a time when world depression was imminent.

Protestants are taken to task for keeping a low profile in public controversies, but they are owed a debt for their creation of the Irish Literary Renaissance and for pioneering the language revival. They are still at work. Avoiding controversy, they have given us our best painters and shown their love of the real Ireland in such books as Robert Lloyd Praeger's *The Way That I Went*. And they and their fellow Catholics are still at their pioneering work, not only in literature, but also in the day-to-day lives of ordinary people in the villages, towns and cities of Ireland.

Terence de Vere White

Above A cottage window at Ballymascanlon, County Louth, surrounded by a profusion of flowers.

Left Lough Leane in Killarney is a famous beauty spot in southern Ireland.

The valley below Glenariff in County Antrim slopes gently down to the sea.

Left A colorful quilt is left hanging
over the fence to dry.

Above Children play by a wall
covered with graffiti in west Belfast.

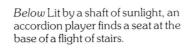

Below Lit by a shaft of sunlight, an accordion player finds a seat at the base of a flight of stairs.

Left Squabbling for scraps, seagulls cluster around two fishing boats moored at Killybegs in County Donegal.

Left Beara peninsula in County Cork.

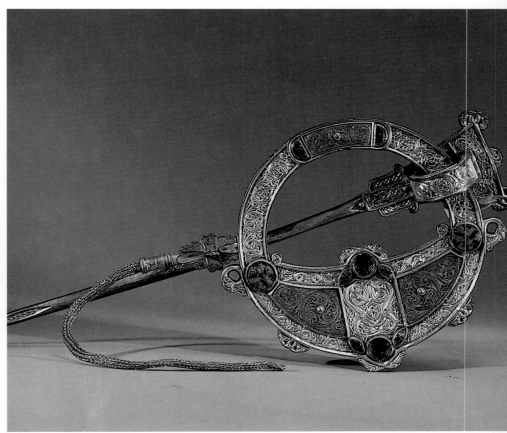

Above The eighth-century Tara brooch, made of cast silver-gilt and beautifully ornamented, is housed in the National Museum of Ireland in Dublin.

This cottage in central Ireland has had the original thatched roof replaced with one made of slate.

Sunset over the River Liffey in Dublin. James Joyce called this river "Anna Livia".

ATLANTIC OCEAN

Tory Island

DONEGAL

Killybegs

Lough Foyle

Giant's Causeway

Derry (Londonderry)

LONDONDERRY

Foyle

Bann

ANTRIM

Carrickfergus

TYRONE

Lough Neagh

Lagan

Belfast

Lough Erne

Enniskillen

ULSTER

Armagh

DOWN

Dundrum

Dromore

△Ben Bulben

LEITRIM

Sligo

FERMANAGH

ARMAGH

MONAGHAN

SLIGO

Achill Island

MAYO

CONNACHT

CAVAN

LOUTH

△Croagh Patrick

ROSCOMMON

LONGFORD

New Grange

Monasterboice

Mellifont

Drogheda

Kells

MEATH

△Tara

DUBLIN

Clifden

GALWAY

Athlone

WESTMEATH

Boyne

Trim

Dunboyne

Maynooth

Galway

Clonmacnoise

Clonfert

OFFALY

Liffey

Dublin

Galway Bay

Shannon

LEINSTER

KILDARE

Aran Islands

Lisdoonvarna

WICKLOW

Glendalough

Lough Derg

LAOIS

CLARE

Durrow

Quin

TIPPERARY

KILKENNY

CARLOW

IRISH SEA

Limerick

Kilkenny

Enniscorthy

LIMERICK

Suir

Cashel

Jerpoint Abbey

Listowel

Clonmel

WEXFORD

Wexford

Tintern Abbey

Dingle Peninsula

Gallarus Oratory

Dingle

KERRY

MUNSTER

Doneraile

Waterford

WATERFORD

Slea Head

Killarney

Blackwater

Lough Leane

△The Paps

The Skelligs

Blarney

Cork

Lee

CORK

Bantry

Bantry Bay

Ancient Ireland

1

Let us dip firstly – and briefly – into Ireland's prehistory. The first people to arrive in Ireland came from Scandinavia to Britain, moving across the narrow strait between Northern Ireland and Scotland, and spreading out to Lough Neagh, to Roscommon, to Carlow and to Limerick.

They came around 6000 BC, and we know little about these middle stone age or mesolithic people. We know nothing about their houses or their graves, and the tools they left were the most primitive flint instruments, found in garbage dumps on the edges of swamps from which they got their food. At that time Ireland was covered by dense woodland, except for its lakes and rivers.

By the year 3000 BC the first farmers had arrived. These neolithic people were almost entirely self-sufficient: they were hunters, potters, even axe-manufacturers, mass producing and exporting axes over 5000 years ago. They had elaborate religious rituals, and raised enormous burial monuments for their dead: megalithic tombs and passage graves, the stones elaborately decorated with spirals, zigzags and whorls.

About the year 2000 BC, following a further great technological advance in the Middle East, the first prospectors and metal-workers

Left A cottage nestles among the walls of the ancient stone fort of Dun Conor on the Aran Islands, off the west coast of Ireland.

Below New Grange, a passage grave overlooking the Boyne river valley in County Meath, is one of Europe's most impressive prehistoric monuments, dating from 2500 BC. The Gaels regarded this pre-Celtic tumulus as an Otherworld divine dwelling. This view shows the north side of New Grange and one of the two stone basins within.

reached the island, ushering in the bronze age, leaving behind pottery vessels finely crafted and exquisitely decorated.

By the year 600 BC, the production of iron had advanced on the continent, and several tribes, skilled in the production and deployment of iron, were establishing themselves in Europe. These peoples – led by rich and powerful chiefs – spoke the same language, Celtic, the forerunner of the Irish spoken in Ireland today. The Greeks knew them as the *Keltoi*, or Celts.

The Celts stretched through the heartland of the continent, from Bohemia to Austria and southern Germany, Switzerland and the eastern borders of France. This confederation of tribes – linked by language, religion and culture – emerged as the first civilization north of the Alps. At the height of their influence (just before 300 BC) they stretched from Finisterre to the Black Sea, and from the North Sea to the Mediterranean. They lacked cohesion and never forged even a state, let alone an empire, nor did they ever achieve ethnic unity.

But over seven centuries of cultural dominance, they most certainly laid the economic, social and artistic foundations of northern European civilization. They invented chain armor, introduced the Greeks and Romans to soap, and were the first to put shoes on horses. They were the first with the iron plowshare and the rotary flour mill, and they pioneered women's rights thousands of years before feminists found a pulpit.

But their real passion was war. In war, the Celts would strut arrogantly before the enemy, their hair stiffened with lime, brandishing their arms, boasting their prowess, bellowing scorn and abuse. Diodorus Siculus, the Greek historian, tells us they beheaded their victims and tied the heads to the necks of their horses. "They embalm in cedar oil the heads of the most distinguished enemies and preserve them carefully in a chest and display them with pride to strangers."

"The whole race," wrote the Greek geographer Strabo, "is madly fond of war."

The whole race was also madly fond of eating and drinking. When they weren't fighting, hunting, wrestling, or chariot-racing, they would gather in a chieftain's house, sprawl on their animal furs, and "drink and eat themselves into a stupor or a state of madness", according to Diodorus.

By 150 BC, they were well established in all parts of Ireland, and in establishing themselves – deliberately or by attrition – they wiped out almost all traces of the peoples who preceded them. The culture and traditions of the mesolithic hunters and the neolithic farmers, of the bronze age metal workers and of the herdsmen, all faded. By the time Irish history properly begins – in the fifth century AD – all of the people of Ireland were utterly Celticized, sharing a common Celtic culture and a common language: they were the Gaels and Gaelic was their language. They were fey, ribald and superstitious, they enjoyed fighting and took palpable pleasure from melancholy, and their powerful imagination had already fashioned and fine-detailed one of the mostly richly varied mythologies of Europe.

It would be foolhardy to attempt to pinpoint when the great Irish myths and sagas evolved. That would be an impossible task: the stories had their genesis in the impermeable mists of Irish prehistory and developed through centuries of oral rendition, naturally resulting in distortion, accretion, duplication and even contradiction.

The Celts loved a story. *The Voyage of Bran* tells how an Ulster king was told a story by his *file,* or poet, every winter night from Samhain (Halloween), to Beltene, or the first day of May. It's possible that the *fili* memorized entire tales, but it's more likely that they knew the outlines and extemporized the minutiae, though later graduates of the Bardic schools were expected to master literally hundreds of classical stories.

It wasn't until the seven, eighth and following centuries that learned Irishmen – mostly monks – began to transcribe the great stories, and this mutation also caused disfigurement and historical corruption. It's true that nothing connected with the Irish myths and sagas is "incontrovertible", in any proper sense, but it's equally true that there was an underlying determination on the part of the scribes to fashion for Ireland a history on the models of the Bible and of Greece and Rome, what historian John MacNeill called "synthetic Irish history". These men in their spartan monasteries spent hour after cramp-inducing hour transmuting the oral to the written, leaving Ireland a legacy lost to almost every other Celtic group.

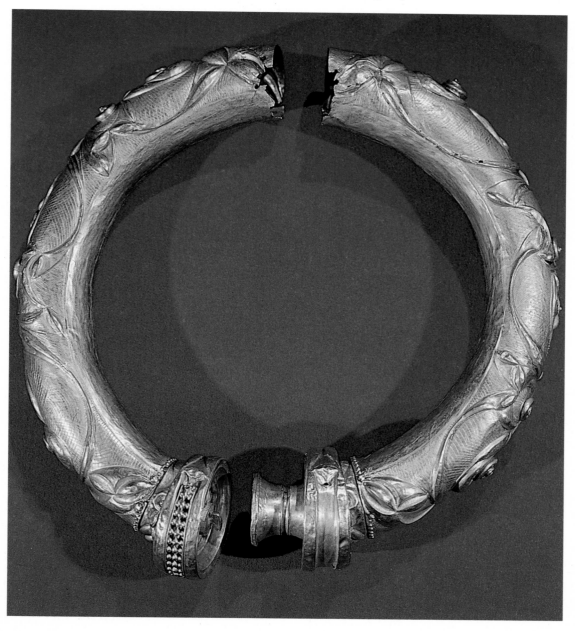

Far Left The Hill of Tara (High Place of the Kings) in County Meath was used as a pagan religious site by the Gaels. A ritual marriage feast, *Feis Temhra,* which confirmed the status of a new king, was held here until the sixth century AD. Many Irish myths and legends are centered around these ancient earthworks.

Left Gold torcs or collars were worn by the images of Gaelic gods and by the heroes of legend. This beautifully ornamented large gold torc (*c.* first century BC) comes from Broighter in County Derry, and is now in the National Museum of Ireland, Dublin.

So what are these great tales? What is so magnificent about these stories that they should be deemed worthy of transcription a thousand years ago, and still be thought worthy of publication as we approach the end of the second millennium AD?

Tradition and convention have ordained that the stories be divided into four cycles: *The Mythological Cycle*, whose stories are set mainly around Tara and the burial mounds of the Boyne Valley; *The Ulster Cycle*, also known as the *Cuchulainn Cycle*, wherein we meet the paradigm of Irish heroes, and which details the allegedly historical events in Ulster some centuries before or after the birth of Christ; *The Kings Cycle*, which concentrates on the (again purportedly historical) kings; and *The Fenian* or *Ossianic Cycle*, concerning Fionn MacCumhail and his adventures with his band of roving warriors.

While these groupings are convenient, it should be remembered that the manuscripts themselves do not justify such cycles, nor is there any chronological justification for them – they are modern and artificial, but, as we have said, they are convenient.

For our knowledge of the earliest mythology, we are indebted to the twelfth century *Leabhar Gabhala Eireann*, or the *Book of Invasions*, which describes six invasions of the island. The first of these happened before the Deluge and was led by Banbha, also one of the earliest names for Ireland. Next came Partholawn, who fought the first battle ever in Ireland against the demonic Fomhorians. Partholawn cleared four plains, built the first guest house, brewed the first beer (Oh, wise Partholawn!) and established legal suretyship, and for all of these good things he and his people perished in a plague.

Next to arrive were the even more hapless followers of Nemhedh, who were under the

Left The Giant's Causeway is an extraordinary natural geological phenomenon, constructed from an overflow of molten lava that split into a collection of three- to nine-sided basalt columns as it cooled. Legend has it that the causeway, which sticks out 200 yards into the sea off the northern coast of Ireland, was built by Fionn MacCumhail so that the Scottish giant, Benandonner, would not get his feet wet before their fight.

Below Found during potato digging in 1867 near Ardagh, County Limerick, the eighth-century Ardagh Chalice has filigree ornamentation of great intricacy and delicacy. (National Museum of Ireland, Dublin.)

25

In Gaelic mythology, Ben Bulben in County Sligo is where Diarmuid was slain by the magic boar of the mountain, who had once been Diarmuid's foster brother. More recently, Yeats is buried in the nearby graveyard at Drumcliff:

Under bare Ben Bulben's head
In Drumcliff churchyard Yeats is laid.
                    W. B. Yeats

thumb of the Fomhorians and were eventually driven out, but not before more plains were created and the island had become a geographical entity, with "local habitation and a name".

The Fir Bolg followed, dividing the country into five provinces – Ulster, Leinster, Munster, Connacht and Meath. They also introduced the notion of kingship, before the next invasion by the Tuatha De Danann (The People of the Goddess Dana). These people fought and triumphed over the Fir Bolg at the first Battle of Moytura, but were then forced into epic conflict with the ancient enemy, the terrible Fomhorians.

bottomless cauldron, a kind of Celtic Jupiter; Angus, his son, the god of youth and love; Dian Ceacht, the god of healing; Goibniu the gods' artificer. And Lugh of the Long Arm, under whose direction the others crafted the mighty weapons, lifted and hurled the Irish mountains, hid the lakes and rivers, and cast showers of fire.

Not all of the stories in the *Book of Invasions* are as monstrously bloody as the *Second Battle of Moytura*, but they are all imbued with the same wondrous mixture of the magical, the supernatural, the fantastic, where exaggeration is the norm, and where people and events bear tenuous (or no) links with reality.

Above The Paps of Anu in County Kerry are named after the goddess Anu or Dana, who was known as the mother of the gods. She is especially associated with the province of Munster, its land and fertility.

The Second Battle of Moytura is mythologically the most important of all the stories in the *Book of Invasions*. The Tuatha De Danann – a pre-Christian pantheon of Gods – confronted and utterly vanquished the evil and demonic Fomhorians (literally "under-demons"). The manner of their triumph and the personalities of the deities are perfect manifestations of the pagan Irish gods and their feats. (And, incidentally, of their nature, for they are not, like their Greek counterparts, awesomely dreadful, brutal and unforgiving. As Aodh de Blacam has remarked, in the literature they are "mighty but friendly beings who share with mankind the adventure of life".)

Dana, the ever-fertile mother-goddess; Dagda the droll, with his mighty club and

It is well to remember that all the stories in the *Book of Invasions* lead up to the arrival in Ireland of the Sons of Mil, the Milesians, who defeated the Tuatha De Danann, and whose descendants, the Gaels, were ever afterwards the dominant people of Ireland. It was the Gaels who composed the narrative and on them fell the responsibility for imposing on it a continuity, an evolution, a binding of the different races into a nation. This they did and well, but with one remarkable omission – the Celts left no myth of the creation of the world or, if they did, it was gently expunged by the Christian literati who were not unprejudiced in these matters, and wished the history of Ireland to be not totally out of line with the Bible and various historians like Eusebius and Orosius,

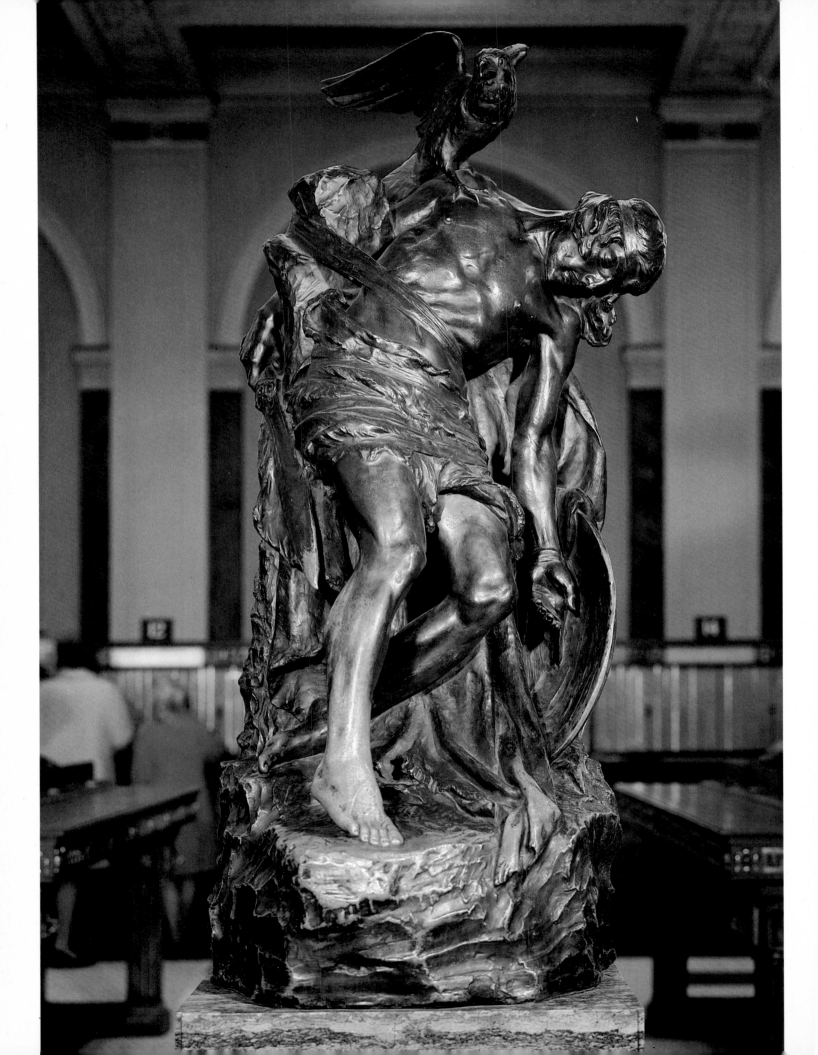

whose views were distinctly Christian.

So it was the Gaels who composed *The Second Battle of Moytura*, and also another story in the *Book of Invasions. The Wooing of Etain* relates how the lovely Etain is wooed and won by Midir in the Otherworld, is changed into a fly by her rival Fuamnach and blown into this world where she is thrice reborn before being wooed back again into the Otherworld by Midir.

This Celtic Otherworld is not the silent, gloomy, classical underworld, peopled by shades, pale, mute and sullen. On the contrary: it is Elysian, a place of innocent love, of beautiful women, of enchanted music. It is sometimes under the ground, sometimes under the sea, sometimes far across the sea; it is the land of the perpetually young, the land of the immortal, the land of the women; it is the land of tranquility and peace. And yet, with the inevitable paradox, its inhabitants fight each other and – a recurring motif throughout the history of Irish literature – may have their feuds resolved by a human, as when Cuchulainn is called upon to help Labhraidh of the Swift Sword-hand, to be rewarded with the love of the beautiful Fann.

Cuchulainn is the great hero of Ulster, the man in the gap against the loathed Connachtaigh, and the protagonist of the *Tain Bo Cuailgne (The Cattle Raid of Cuailgne)*, the magnificent central saga of *The Ulster Cycle*, This cycle has as much violence as the previous one, but it is more logically rooted. Although the feats are as outrageously exaggerated, the hero (while seemingly omnicompetent) is nevertheless vulnerable, a sort of Celtic Achilles. The story of the Tain is the story of a row about cattle, a universal saga and one that continues to this day.

Queen Maeve of Connacht covets the Brown Bull of Cuailgne in Ulster so that she may have a bull as powerful as her husband's. Ulster is not lightly attacked by her enemies – nor is she still – but suddenly the Ulster warriors are struck down by an illness which makes them as "weak and helpless as a woman in childbirth". All, that is, except Setanta, or Cuchulainn (the Hound of Culainn) as he has since been renamed.

Left The bronze statue of the heroic death of Cuchulainn was erected in the General Post Office, Dublin, after the Republic of Ireland was declared in 1916.

Below Achill Head in County Mayo, off the west coast of Ireland.

He defends Ulster with magnificent energy and valor, even (and finally) against his foster-brother and best friend, Ferdia, who crossed over to the side of the Connachtaigh and was cajoled by Maeve into confronting Cuchulainn. But what chance had Ferdia against a warrior who was subject to the *riastradh*, or battle-frenzy? The description of this battle frenzy leaves little wonder that once, at the sight of Cuchulainn's frenzy, one hundred of Maeve's warriors fell dead from horror. Still, he was brought down and took his last breath having tied himself to a pillar-stone, so that he might die standing and not lying down.

Thus departed Cuchulainn, greatest of the Red Branch knights, mightiest of the mighty, the quintessential Irish mythic hero: barbaric, poetical, full of boastful rant, proud, fearless and contradictory, vulnerable to grief, and choosing one brief hour of immortalizing glory rather than an eternity of tedious worthiness.

Other stories in the *Cycle* are hard put to match the wild, aristocratic grandeur of the *Tain*, but they are none the less splendid for that. For instance, the chief of the preliminary stories to the *Tain*, Deirdre and the Sons of Usna, is pure romantic tragedy, and moves towards its resolution with the inexorable logic of the tragedies of Shakespeare or Sophocles.

It tells how Deirdre's fatal beauty was coveted by the aged King Conor, but she fell in love with Naoise, the son of Usna, and eloped with him to Scotland, together with his brothers Ainle and Ardan. But they were enticed back to Ireland and brought to their doom partly because of Naoise's masculine contempt for a woman's intuition. When Conor broke his oath and had the three sons of Usna beheaded, he took Deirdre by force. One day, out on the chariot with Deirdre and Owen of Duracht, Conor said: "Deirdre, what is it that you hate most of all on earth?" And she replied, "Thou thyself and Owen of Duracht". And Conor said, "Deirdre, the glance of thee between me and Owen is like the glance of a ewe between rams". And Deirdre threw herself headfirst from the chariot, smashed her skull against a rock, and died – and in her life and death inspired more Irish writing than any other mythic female, from Yeats and James Stephens to Synge and Lady Gregory.

The centerpiece of *The Ulster Cycle* is the great Emhain Macha, seat of the Ulster kings, near present-day Armagh. The Red Branch knights were taught their skills inside its trenches and ramparts, great feasts were held within its walls, and it was there, during the long winter nights, that the *fili* recited the epic narratives, fashioned and shaped by genera-tion after generation of their successors into the legends that survive today.

The *fili* were powerful. Their power rested in their ability with words, particularly satirical words. These struck mortal fear into the hearts of the most powerful of men, even the kings,

Left The River Shannon near Athlone in County Westmeath, at the heart of Ireland, is so called after the loins of a bull, Ath Luain, literally the "Ford of the Loins" This comes from the *Tain Bo Cuailgne*, the tale of Queen Maeve's invasion of Ulster in pursuit of the Brown Bull of Cuailgne.

Above Over 300 ogham stones survive in Ireland, mostly in the southern counties. This one is at Kilnakedur in County Kerry. Ogham script, the earliest form of Irish, is a secret writing derived from the Latin and used for inscriptions cut into the edges of stones.

who were the solid fountainheads of the social order. The king stories, while they are imbued with all the heroism of *The Ulster Cycle*, nevertheless have a different emphasis: they are concerned more with the status and function of the sacral kingship than with the heroic values and ideals.

The great Cormac MacAirt, who died in 266 AD, is the prime exemplar of the kingly gifts. That he should be valorous, energetic and of sublime sensibility goes without saying, but such virtues would not mark him off from a thousand knights. He must also deliver, and be seen to deliver, judgements of unquestionable disinterestedness. When Conaire Mor – a compassionate king whose reign ushered in tranquility and prosperity – exhibited a more than just share of mercy when dealing with his foster-brothers, he sparks off a reaction that moves him ineluctably to his own death in a welter of violence, as we learn in the tragic story of *The Destruction of the Hostel of Da Derga*. Quite a different emphasis is to be found in *Ronan's Killing of His Own Kin*. When Maol Fhothartaigh, Son of Ronan, King of Leinster, spurns the advances of his father's young wife, she destroys him with her jealous anger.

The king stories show a distinct de-emphasizing of the hero as a hero and personality, but underline the status of the hero as a king whose heroism manifests itself not so much in the triumphs of combat, but in the exercise of social responsibility and in the

Right Poulnabrone Dolmen in the Burren, near Ballyraughan, County Clare, is a portal dolmen where the dead were buried. It consists of a chamber formed by three or more upright stones and roofed by a single capstone. Originally, dolmens were covered by a mound of earth. Every dolmen in Ireland is known as "Diarmuid and Grainne's Bed" – an allusion to the tale of Grainne's elopement with Diarmuid and their flight from the vengeance of Fionn.

recognition of kingship as the paramount institution in Irish society, to be fought for, achieved, and lived up to.

In *The Fenian* or *Ossianic Cycle*, we are back once more in the spirit of the wilderness, with Fionn MacCumhail and the Fianna, a band of professional warriors without tribal loyalty, rootless and mobile, yet recognized as serving a valid function: they defend Ireland against its enemies, whether from within or without or from the Otherworld. They roam the length and breadth of the island, hunting, fishing, fighting, falling in love, continuously communing with and marveling at every aspect of nature.

Over the centuries, *The Ossianic Cycle* displaced *The Ulster Cycle* in popularity, and

Fionn and Oisin and Diarmuid and Grainne became known universally as Cuchulainn never did. Perhaps it was because of the great love story of Diarmuid and Grainne (every dolmen in Ireland is known as "Diarmuid and Grainne's Bed") which is analogous to the romance of Tristan and Iseult; perhaps because the feats of Fionn and his warriors are not so wildly improbable and therefore more sympathetic to the contemporary mind; or perhaps because of the constant and lyric evocation of their love for nature.

Whatever the reason, or combination of reasons, the *Ossianic* tales swept Europe in the eighteenth century, and permeated European art and life in a way that the Irish vernacular tradition would not do again for almost 200

Below Many examples of early Irish masonry can be found on White Island and Devenish Island on the shores of Lough Erne in County Fermanagh. Through this arch can be seen a human mask and eight other odd figures built into the church wall. One figure is an abbot, but the others are thought to be early Irish soldiers or warriors.

Top Right Gallarus Oratory on the Dingle peninsula in County Kerry is the largest surviving stone oratory of the early Christian church. The Oratory is built with dry-stone walls and a corbeled roof; a shape typical of ancient building methods.

Bottom Right The Skellig Islands off the south coast of County Kerry are where the monks of the early Irish Church lived their ascetic lives of self-denial. The Skelligs were raided by Vikings, but were not finally abandoned until early in the thirteenth century.

Below Croagh Patrick, literally Patrick's Mountain, is in County Mayo on the Atlantic coast. Ever since St Patrick fasted and prayed here during Lent in 441 AD, Croagh Patrick has been the scene of an annual pilgrimage in July, which evolved from the pagan festival of Lugansa, marking the end of summer.

years. A Scotsman named James MacPherson based his poems *Fingal* and *Temora* on *The Ossianic Cycle.* MacPherson claimed they were written by Ossian (Oisin) and found and translated by himself.

It was a magnificent fraud, but it fooled the Edinburgh literati (except for David Hume) and, for a while, their London counterparts. And it bowled over the Europeans. Goethe compared Ossian to Shakespeare. Napoleon read the poems and his marshal, Bernadotte, brought them to Sweden and gave the name Oscar to successive Swedish kings (and, would you believe, gave the names Oscar *and* Fingal to the son of the court physician, Dr Wilde).

Meanwhile, Ossian's genius pervaded European art. Ossianic themes were painted by Angelica Kaufmann and Abilgard the Dane. The French painters Gerard, Girodet and Ingres painted massive pictures which mixed the Fianna warriors and Napoleon's soldiers, and those pictures hung in the imperial apartments in Paris and Rome.

One of the outstanding stories in *The Ossianic Cycle* is the *Colloquy of the Ancients,* in which the last great pagan heroes of the Fianna, Oisin and Caoilte, converse at length

with Ireland's first Christian bishop, St Patrick. The "tonsured one" had at last arrived, and thus do the myths and sagas knit themselves into the true history of Ireland.

Patrick arrived in Ireland in the middle of the fifth century, and is the author of the earliest documents known to have been written on the island. So it is with him that Irish history really begins. In his own words, he "baptized thousands, ordained clerics everywhere, gave presents to kings, was put in irons, lived in daily expectation of murder, treachery and captivity, journeyed everywhere in many dangers, and rejoiced to see the flock of the Lord in Ireland growing splendidly with the greatest care and the sons and daughters of kings becoming monks and virgins of Christ".

The conversion to Christianity was rapid. Patrick set up an episcopal system of Church government, but he also, more importantly, introduced the monastic life to the island, and was gratified by the large numbers of his new converts who embraced it. Within two centuries of his death Ireland had become unique in western Christendom in having its most important churches ruled by a monastic hierarchy. Monasteries were sited all over the island

and constituted the earliest settlements of people. They were nothing like the later great monasteries. Life was austere, rules were strict, and the life of each monk was a continuing act of self-denial.

In the monasteries, the copying of manuscripts was an important occupation. The elite among the monks were the scribes: the libraries and scriptoria had manuscripts suspended in satchels by leather straps from the walls, and an ample supply of writing materials — waxed tablets, parchment, quills, stylos and inkhorns.

And in these monasteries, the great myths of the Gaels were written down for the first time. Not all of them have survived the centuries — some were lost; some were hidden, never to be found. Others were destroyed in the flames that engulfed monasteries when they were attacked by the Irish. And others were burnt by the marauders of the seventh invasion of Ireland — the Vikings.

David Hanly

Fair Haired Foreigners and Dark Haired Natives

2

The country that the Vikings began to invade from the seventh century onwards, and that the Normans invaded in the twelfth century, was quiet and green; an island on the edge of the world. It had escaped the invasions of the Romans and barbarians; indeed, the customs and way of life of its Celtic inhabitants had hardly changed in the previous thousand years.

At that time, Ireland contained at least a hundred small kingdoms, made up of closely related families living within the protection of earthen ring forts in wattle houses thatched in straw, rearing crops and tending cattle. Towns or great centers of power and trade did not exist; they made treaties, healed quarrels, traded with foreign merchants and held singing and poetry contests at seasonal fairs and festivals. They fought over cattle or women, rarely over territory.

Art was literary rather than graphic. The *file* was a wise man and privileged, whose function it was to preserve tradition and the genealogies of the royal and noble families, and to expound and record the law. The *fili* presided at the inauguration of kings. They wrote poems to praise or condemn; they had the power of words. Instead of the free creative inspiration of the modern poet, the *fili* claimed a traditional semi-magical authority with may have descended to them from the ancient Druids.

The one intrusion into the seamless pattern of Irish life was the coming of Christianity. Far from uniting Ireland with the rest of Europe as might be expected, this produced that singularly isolated and very peculiar organization, the early Irish church.

The Christian church that St Patrick founded in the fifth century showed, in its simpler forms, the complex legal structures that the church had borrowed from the Roman Empire. The saint set up a territorial episcopate; a structure of church discipline with canon law controlling such important matters as clerical celibacy, marriage rules and the independent property rights of the church.

Monks and monasteries were all under proper ecclesiastical authority even if they had some exotic hermetical practices borrowed from Egypt. In the intervening centuries between the Viking raids and the Norman invasion, the Irish church developed and continued to practice its own peculiar forms. Instead of bishops there were abbots, many of them laymen, ruling the church. An hereditary clergy

Left The monastery of Clonmacnoise on the banks of the River Shannon was founded by St Ciaran in the sixth century.

Above An early Irish grave slab from Clonmacnoise.

Below A "carpet" page from the exquisitely decorated Book of Durrow containing the four Gospels in Latin, which was composed by monks in County Offaly during the seventh century.

evolved which held the many monasteries and their lands as the property of their families or clans. In matters of morals the church did not often intervene; marriage, for example, was a secular issue. Parishes and parish structures did not exist – and besides, the married clergy were far too busy with their farms and families to serve them.

This cozy compromise which was the Irish

church existed from the eighth century onwards. Although not fanatically celibate, the monks were not immoral. Nor did they lack learning; in fact, they had largely taken over the role of the *fili*, preserving saga tales and genealogies, recording them for the first time. They also produced a large body of biblical commentary and religious verse as well as some delightful nature lyrics. The short story

writer Frank O'Connor had a soft spot for the civilization of this period, which he aptly describes as that of the "little monasteries".

The rulers of the monasteries, having disposed of the Romantist prigs, are no longer the harsh unwordly men we meet in the pages of Bede, who read nothing but their gospels and Psalm books. They are far more like the parsons of Peacock and Meredith – wealthy, worldly, scholarly men who live in the little oases of civilization among the bogs and the woods, in comfortable wooden houses with wine cellars and libraries, with clever sons who will become in their turn abbots or professors of scripture, and clever daughters who will manage big convents or marry among the ruling classes.

Below Remains of the tenth-century Viking settlement being uncovered in Wood Quay, Dublin, during recent archeological excavations.

They are custodians of relics and treasures worth the ransom of a great many kings.

Though one can cast some doubt on the monastic wine cellars in O'Connor's version, there is no doubt about the treasures, and it was these very treasures that lured the Vikings to turn the Arcadian dream of Irish history into a nightmare.

The Norse raiders struck suddenly from the sea in their light, swift boats, equipped with that new invention, the keel. In 795 they burned the church of Lambay Island off Dublin and attacked two island monasteries, Inishmurray and Inishboffin off the west coast. Why monasteries? Well, there were no towns or centers of population and the monasteries were comparatively rich with portable wealth such as relics in shrines of precious metal, decorated book shrines, and altar vessels of gold and silver.

The raids on island and coastal monasteries continued for about 40 years. Then the Vikings began to strike more boldly inland, deep into the heart of the country, sending fleets up the Boyne, the Liffey and, above all, the Shannon. From these raids, they could reach the rich monasteries of Clonmacnoise, Birr and Seir. In 840, the Vikings started to build ship shelters along the coast, and by 841 wintered for the first time in Dublin. Gradually, over two centuries, these Viking forts became the first Irish towns. The Viking towns of Stangford, Dublin, Wicklow, Wexford, Waterford, Cork and Limerick mushroomed along the east and south coasts.

Unlike their Danish brothers in England or France, where they became the civic-minded Normans, the Irish Vikings did not seek land. Instead, piracy gave way to trade and industry. Newly excavated Viking Dublin reveals industrial zones of shoemakers, combmakers, metal workers and potters.

Towns and their hinterlands were the Viking sphere of influence; the largest territory they held was the coastal plain from north Dublin to Wicklow. They intermarried with Irish families, joined them in internecine warfare and, under the more harmless name of Ostmen, formed a small but important component of Irish society.

The Norse raiders gave the Irish civilization in the form of towns, coinage, and the arts of fishing and shipping. On the negative side,

Below Ardmore round tower in County Waterford is one of the many medieval stone towers which are found on monastic sites in Ireland. They were probably originally used as bell-towers.

Left Glendalough ("The Glen of Two Lakes") is a favorite beauty spot in the Wicklow Hills. St Kevin's Church is named after the seventh-century hermit who founded the monastery there.

Above The tenth-century Cross of Muiredach at Monasterboice, County Louth, is carved with traditional biblical scenes, and is considered to be one of Ireland's finest high crosses.

their violence and destruction broke up the cozy framework of Irish society. Violence replaced the restraints of society and customary law. The overlordships which developed in response to Viking attacks added a new element of violent competitiveness to Irish society. This, in turn, never allowed any overlord to become so strong that a countrywide power could be established to resist the next challenge – that of the Normans.

During their Irish sojourn, the Ostmen of the Irish towns had become Christian. When bishops were appointed, English-trained monks who owed allegiance to Canterbury were chosen, rather than Irish priests. These, with a few reforming Irish bishops based in Munster, established contact with the reformist continental church of Gregory the Great. This began a series of reforming synods in the first half of the twelfth century which took on the ambitious task of internal reform of the Irish church. They set up a system of territorial dioceses presided over by bishops. Four metropolitan archbishoprics were created; Armagh the primacy, Dublin, Cashel and Tuam, with a series of suffragan sees under them. On paper, at least, the Irish church took the form it still maintains.

The work of reform was much helped by the introduction of the continental orders of monks. The Cistercians were introduced into Ireland by Malachy, the saintly and reforming bishop of Armagh, mostly through his friendship with their founder, Bernard of Clairvaux. The first foundation at Mellifont commenced in 1142 and within 50 years it had hived off 20 communities. The canons regular of St Augustine also introduced by Malachy were even more prolific and before the end of the century the two orders between them had superseded the older Celtic monasteries.

In spite of these reforms, Rome was dissatisfied with the self-healing progress of the Irish church. This is the only way one can interpret the action of Pope Adrian IV (the one and only English pope, as the Irish are quick to point out) who in 1155 "granted and donated Ireland" to the English King Henry II. The Pope's motives are spelled out by his intimate friend and fellow countryman John of Salisbury:

In response to my petition the Pope granted and donated Ireland to the illustrious English King, Henry II, to be held by him and his successors as his letters still testify. He did this by that right of longstanding from the Donation of Constantine whereby all islands are said to belong to the Roman Church. Through me the Pope sent a gold ring set with a magnificent emerald as a sign that he had invested the King with the right to rule Ireland; it was later ordered that this ring be kept in the public treasury.

Irish historians have frequently thrown

Far Left The first Cistercian monastery in Ireland was founded by St Malachy at Mellifont, County Louth, in 1142. This picture shows one of its more unusual features, an octagonal lavabo where the monks used to wash.

Left St Brendan founded a monastery at Clonfert, County Galway, in the sixth century, but the present cathedral dates from the twelfth century. The west doorway is decorated with human heads and marigolds.

Above Cormac's Chapel, dating back to the twelfth century, is the earliest surviving building on the Rock of Cashel, County Tipperary.

doubt on the very existence, not to say validity, of the papal bull *Laudabiliter*, which was reputed to give formal expression to this arbitrary gift to an English king by an English pope. Whatever the legal facts, certainly this feeling of the necessity of reforming the Irish was held not only in England but in Rome. Even a favorable witness like Bernard of Clairvaux felt that something must be done about Ireland. Writing about Malachy's task in Ireland Bernard says:

Never had he found men so shameless in their morals, so wild in their rites, so impious in their faith, so barbarous in their laws, so stubborn in discipline, so unclean in their life. They were Christians in name; in fact they were pagans. They did not give first fruits or tithes; they did not enter on lawful marriage; they made no confessions; nowhere was there to be found any who might either seek or impose penance. Ministers of the altar were few indeed. But what need was there of more when even the few lived idle lives among the laity.

That Bernard is overstating his case there we can gather from the contrast he describes when Malachy set fruitfully to work: "Churches were rebuilt and a clergy appointed to them: the sacraments were duly solemnized and confessions were made: the people came to church, and those who were living in concubinage were united in lawful wedlock". That was the intention, but the record shows that a long time was to pass before such an orderly state was achieved.

In fact the Norman arrival in Ireland had little to do with church reform: they simply took sides for mercenary motives in an Irish domestic quarrel.

Dermot MacMurrough, the King of Leinster, found himself on the losing side in an Irish tribal fight with the O'Connor overlords of Connaught and particularly with one of O'Connor's henchmen, Tighernan O'Rourke, whose wife MacMurrough had kidnapped in a previous campaign. He fled abroad and sought help from Henry II of England. In spite of his grants and bulls from the Pope, Henry showed little interest. Instead he referred Dermot to some of his under-employed Welsh knights, in particular Richard de Clare, Earl of Pembroke (known to Irish history as Strongbow), and to a wild Norman-Welsh clan, "the sons of Nesta", who became the Geraldines of Irish history. Strongbow was bribed by Dermot MacMurrough with the offer of his daughter's hand in marriage and the succession to the rich kingdom of Leinster.

Small forces of Norman knights, Welsh archers and Flemish mercenaries trickled quietly into Ireland. Strongbow himself arrived

Below Gerald of Wales (Giraldus Cambrensis), visiting Ireland in the wake of the Norman invasion of 1170, considered the Irish people barbaric and glorified the conquest. This illustration from his manuscript "History and Topography of Ireland" shows the composition of a book at Kildare. (British Library.)

Left Brian Boru was crowned in 977 at "Royal and Saintly Cashel", stronghold of the kings of Munster. Tradition has it that one of these kings was baptized on the Rock in the fifth century by St Patrick on his way through the Kingdom. The surviving ecclesiastical buildings all date from a later time.

Below "The Marriage of Strongbow and Aoife" by the Victorian painter Daniel Maclise shows the King of Leinster marrying his daughter to the Norman invader the Earl of Pembroke in order to secure military assistance. (National Gallery of Ireland.)

Right William Marshall founded Tintern Abbey in about 1200 in thanks for a safe crossing from England. The first monks were Welsh Cistercians from the parent abbey in Monmouthshire. After the dissolution of the monasteries part of the church was converted into a three-story house and was inhabited until 1960.

Above The magnificent medieval Great Hall at Desmond Castle, Newcastle West, County Limerick, was once the home of the Fitzgeralds. More recently it has been used as a bingo hall.

Below The ruins of another Cistercian monastery at Jerpoint, County Kilkenny. The twelfth-century abbey nave and later tower are seen here from the fifteenth-century cloisters.

with the main force in August 1170 and soon retook Leinster for Dermot and captured the Ostmen's capital of Dublin. With Dermot's death in 1171 he was able to claim his inheritance as King of Leinster.

Henry II at last began to show interest in Ireland when he realized Strongbow and his companions might set up an independent kingdom there. In 1171 he arrived in person to claim the allegiance of his knights and of any of the Irish kings who felt inclined to submit to him, which many did. Churchmen also tendered their loyalty and were rewarded with his encouragement in reforming synods. The Norman invasion of Ireland was now official. This was not, though, a Norman conquest. Because of the peculiar decentralized nature of Irish administration there was really no one overall authority to conquer.

For the next two centuries Norman power fluctuated in Ireland; at its strongest, two-thirds of the country came, directly or indirectly, under Norman sway. But even then that power was exercised only in the Ostman ports, in the new towns like New Ross and Kilkenny which had been set up in the river valleys, and in the advanced castles and garrisons in the west, like Galway and Athenry. Ireland was divided into two societies: the castle and town society of the Normans with its Norman-French language and English law, and the traditional rural society with the Irish language and brehon law.

Intermarriage and contact with the Irish led many Normans to adopt Irish clothes, speech and customs. A parliament held at Kilkenny in 1366 set out to correct these abuses bewailing the fact that, "now many English of the said land, forsaking the English language, fashion, manner of riding, laws and usages, live and govern themselves by the manners, fashions and language of the Irish enemy, and have made divers marriages and alliances between themselves and the Irish enemies by which the said land and its liege people, the English language and the allegiance due to our lord the King and the English laws are put in subjection and decayed . . ."

In spite of such laws, which were many times repeated, commerce between the two nations continued but they never did become one. In spite of the much-handled phrase about becoming "more Irish than the Irish themselves", the Normans did not become Irish, nor did they succeed. in conquering the Irish. Ireland was now two nations and so in many ways it has continued.

The effects of the Norman invasion are visible even today on the Irish landscape. The Normans were not casual raiders or founders of trading posts like their Viking predecessors; their objective was land and stability. They

Left After the invasion of 1170 the Normans built massive stone fortresses in which to settle down. Hugh de Lacy started building Trim Castle, County Meath, on the banks of the River Boyne in 1180.

Below The Normans founded towns such as New Ross on the River Barrow in river valleys in the southeast of Ireland.

held the land they captured by building castles. At first their castles were temporary affairs, high mounds of earth topped by wooden forts, the motte and bailey of the Bayeux tapestry. Soon, though, they were of stone. In the heart of Dublin, on the seacoast in Carrickfergus, on a rock overlooking Limerick harbor, and above all in the river valleys of Leinster, walled enclosures with drum towers at the corners and often a high circular or square keep in the middle were raised in the green and flat Irish landscape. They dominated whole plains, as in the great castle of Trim in County Meath; they stood at river crossings, such as Bunratty in County Clare.

Under the shelter of these castles, Norman towns grew up with mills and markets. Great churches of the new continental orders were

Below The three-tiered nave of the Anglo-Norman St Patrick's Cathedral in Dublin.

common by the family or tribe rather than claimed by individuals, understood little and cared less for the legal tangle in which they had become enmeshed.

In the fourteenth century, there was an Irish resurgence. The Irish, with the help of mercenaries from Scotland with their long axes, were learning to fight back. The area of Ireland actually controlled by the English government contracted to the Pale, an area of a few counties in Leinster around Dublin.

In the rest of the country, the Irish chieftains were building themselves castles, the tall, rectangular type with bristling Irish battlements that had come into fashion. Like the Normans, they too were endowing abbeys. Increasingly, the new religious foundations were friaries of the mendicant orders, the

Right The two-story round keep at Dundrum Castle, County Down, was probably built at the end of the twelfth century.

built in the towns; the abbeys of Duiske and Tintern in the Leinster river valleys were as English in their style as were the monks that came from English mother houses. Indeed the very stone for their vaults and window dressings were imported from Dundry, near Bristol, and floated on flat boats up the Irish rivers.

Even where they could not possess the land, the Normans claimed it, fiefed it under their feudal system to their supporters – or even to the Irish who actually possessed it – for knights' fee, service and rent. If they could collect, well and good; if not, they at least had their claim on paper. The Irish, with their own laws decreeing that lands should be held in

Franciscans, Dominicans and the Augustinian friars who had begun to replace the old monastic orders in influence. The slim friary belltowers, with their characteristic Irish inward slope or "batter", and the empty triangle of their roof gables rise frequently in the western sky far away from any town or village.

From 1400 on, the Norman settlement in Ireland really went into decline. English kings were too involved in Europe to spare money for an Irish colony and the Wars of the Roses about the Royal succession finally withdrew attention from Ireland.

As so often before, it was one of the great Norman families who filled the power vacuum.

Far Left Dunsoghly Castle in County Dublin is owned by the Dublin Commission of Public Work.

Left The O'Brien castle of Leamaneh, County Clare, was originally just a fifteenth-century tower, but a four-story mansion was added some 200 years later.

Below The ruins of Quin Friary, County Clare, built in 1453.

Below Under Elizabeth I local Irish people were dispossessed and their lands granted to the English. The Lakes of Killarney were given to the Browne family.

Early in the century, James Butler, the fourth Earl of Ormonde, held sway. He ruled the rich lands of Tipperary and Kilkenny and, like all Butlers, was prominent in diplomacy and negotiation rather than battle. He was definitely a king's man. When he died in 1452, his son and heir married an English noblewoman and identified his interests with England, so the Butlers disappeared from Irish history for a long time.

The next family who came to power were the Geraldines of Desmond, the southern branch of the legendary "family of Nesta". They ruled all Munster like a Gaelic kingdom, having not only feudal loyalty from Norman families like the Barrys and the Roches and junior Geraldines like the knights of Glin and Kerry, but they also got recognition from the great Gaelic

families such as the MacCarthys and the O'Sullivans. Thomas, the seventh Earl of Desmond, was more a Gaelic chief than a Norman lord. He held sway from 1461 to 1467 when he was arrested, detained and beheaded. This act drove the Desmond family into rebellion against the crown which continued for the best part of a century. The rebellion was finally defeated under Elizabeth I.

It was now the turn of the Fitzgeralds of Kildare. Garret Mor, the Great Earl of Kildare, came to power in 1477 and, through favor and disfavor, continued in power until the eve of the Tudor reconquest of Ireland in 1513.

The Norman settlers had fixed their towns and castles in the plains, along the seacoast and in the rich accessible river valleys; the highlands, the bogs, the forests and the rich pastures beyond the forests were still Gaelic country offering no loyalty to the English crown. It was these disloyal lands that the Tudor monarchs set out to conquer. They used new methods; surveyors and maps, and trans-

Below This woodcut by John Derricke from his "Image of Irelande", 1570, shows Sir Henry Sidney, one of Elizabeth I's deputies in Ireland, leaving Dublin Castle for a tour of the country. Heads of rebels displayed above the gate served as a warning to others.

plantation instead of feudal grants. They were motivated by religion, to plant the English Reformation in Ireland as well as Tudor colonial expansionism.

The two Irish nations – the Norman settlers and the Gaelic clans – had at least the cause of a common beseiged religion now, but even then they couldn't make political common cause against a new and more effective enemy. The last parliament in Kilkenny, the Confederation of Kilkenny of 1642, tried to use their common elements to unite them against the Puritan parliament. The Duke of Ormonde was, as always, keeping a watchful eye on these proceedings, but Oliver Cromwell and his moss troopers brought the whole proceedings to a murderous close. The Duke of Ormonde surfaced again as the Viceroy after the Restoration, but the Gaelic part of Ireland, landless and proscribed by ever more effective penal laws, went into the long dark of the hidden Ireland.

Sean J. White

Eighteenth and Nineteenth Century Ireland

romwell's soldiers conquered a country that was already devastated by war, famine and plague. His civil administrators followed through with a religious policy that was directed in part against Anglican prelacy, but much more fiercely against the Roman Catholic clergy, who were hunted down. Many were killed.

This period of government under the Protectorate left memories which endured among the ordinary people for many generations. They had to practice their religion in many places by stealth, gathering at "Mass rocks" in out of the way places, protected by look-outs. In the popular memory, the days of Cromwellian persecution were ultimately transferred to a later period, so that the whole episode came to be associated with the later penal laws against Catholicism of the eighteenth century. But the very name of Cromwell passed into folklore as a great bogey.

The Protectorate carried out very extensive confiscations of land. The war had been financed by promising confiscated land to those who took part in it. Large numbers of "delinquent" proprietors were moved across the Shannon, to Connacht and Clare, to

Left The River Foyle at Derry (or Londonderry) looks peaceful enough in the balmy light of evening, but it was the scene of a siege that lasted for three months while the 30,000 starving people within the walls lived on a diet of dogs, cats, mice, candles and leather.

Below In the latter part of the seventeenth century French Huguenot cemetery in Baggot Dublin, followed by Dutch and Flemings, who introduced buildings of brick, such as this Huguenot craftsmen moved to Street, Dublin.

Above In 1649, Cromwell arrived in Ireland to subdue the last remaining Royalists. He attacked Catholic Drogheda and, in one of the blackest events in Irish history, his troops massacred the garrison, clergy and some of the townspeople. This engraving by Barlow dates from the eighteenth century.

receive there estates equivalent to a proportion of the lands they had to leave in the east.

This plantation scheme, under the Act of Settlement, was only partly successful. But the administrators had so much trouble trying to find out who had what land where (so that they could redistribute it) that they were forced to attempt an accurate survey. The so-called "Down Survey" which resulted gives us our first detailed mapping of Ireland.

One of the destabilizing features of Irish politics throughout the seventeenth century had been the great uneasiness of almost all the landlords of the country about the security of their tenure. At a time when common people had little say, if any, in politics, and when the conduct of government and the formation of policy was in the hands of the landed gentry and aristocracy, the widespread uncertainty created by repeated confiscations was probably the largest single influence on the political decisions made by the landlords.

After the death of Cromwell in 1658, politicians in England decided to bring back the king, Charles II, son of the king whom Cromwell had fought and had put to death. This immediately raised crucial questions about the ownership of land. Were the dispossessed and often exiled lords who had been faithful to the crown to get their lands back? Were the Cromwellians who had been given land under the plantation to lose it again? The Restoration of 1660 was based on an attempt at a compromise between the two.

This was more difficult in Ireland than in England. Almost all the landlords were left with one kind of grievance or another. Within the immediate post-Cromwellian period, the old Gaelic order that had survived for a thousand years finally disintegrated. The literature in Irish of this time is full of anger and lament for the passing of the old order. Only a few of the ancient great families – those that had become Protestant – survived in possession of extensive estates, although some of the lesser old Catholic landlords still hung on here and there (the O'Connells, in Kerry, being a good example).

When Charles II died and was succeeded by his brother, James II, in 1685, the effect on Ireland was immediate and disturbing. James was a Roman Catholic, and his accession to the throne raised Catholic hopes for a restoration of confiscated lands and estates, and correspondingly gave rise to Protestant fears of a loss of the same lands. In 1687, James

58

Left The peaceful county town of Wexford, in the southeast of Ireland. The streets once ran with blood when Cromwell's troops slaughtered 2000 inhabitants.

appointed a Catholic, Richard Talbot, Duke of Tyrconnell, as his Lord Lieutenant to govern Ireland. He was a known opponent of the compromise settlement which left the Protestant planters in possession of the lands.

Tyrconnell began replacing Protestants with Catholics in the public service and recruiting Catholics in large numbers into the army. He made it clear that he proposed to undo the settlement. However, in the "Glorious Revolution" of 1688, another English rebellion, this time bloodless, overthrew the king, who fled to France, and brought in his place his daughter Mary (a Protestant) and her husband William of Orange. This was stimulated by the birth of a male heir to the throne, opening the way to a Catholic dynasty. Tyrconnell, however, held Ireland for James.

But not quite all of it. Here and there, the Protestant landowners and settlers acted against him, especially in Ulster. Londonderry and Enniskillen closed their gates against Tyrconnell.

Ireland now became a battlefield in a European war, for the king of France decided to give military support to James II against William III. James landed in the south of Ireland in March 1689 and marched north to Derry, whose governor, Robert Lundy, was just about to open the gates to him when he was overthrown from within the city. The siege of Derry lasted for three months and was finally relieved

Below The Battle of the Boyne, painted by Jan Wyck in 1693, now hangs in the National Gallery of Ireland.

when relief ships got through to the starving population and garrison. It has become one of the great legends of Ulster loyalism.

Soon after the raising of the siege, Marshall Schomberg, King William's commander, landed at Belfast Lough and made a base for the winter at Carrickfergus. In the spring of 1690, 7000 French troops landed in the south to aid King James. In June, King William landed at Carrickfergus and joined Schomberg. They marched south and were met by King James and his forces at the river Boyne, 30 miles north of Dublin, on July 1 (old style – July 12 in our present calendar). Schomberg was killed as he crossed the river, but James, defeated, fled to Dublin, which he soon had to abandon. The war went on for a year, with the Jacobites holding and defending the south and west. After their defeat in the critical battle of Aughrim (County Galway) in 1691, they were besieged in Limerick and finally surrendered, on terms, in October. The military terms of the treaty of Limerick were carried out, but the Protestant parliament which met in Dublin refused to ratify the civil terms.

Instead they proceeded to build a system designed to exclude Roman Catholics from property, power and influence, and also to put pressure on them to accept and conform to the Protestant faith. The further confiscations of land were not complete until the opening years of the eighteenth century. By then, more than

80 per cent of the land of Ireland had changed hands within about a hundred years, and in the process a whole new class of proprietors was established in control of the property and power of the country, without roots in the past. This was what became known as the "Protestant Ascendancy".

The parliament passed a series of laws, known as the "Popery laws" or "penal laws", to restrict to Anglican Protestants the power, property and privilege of the country. Test oaths excluded Catholics and Presbyterians from most public office. The Roman Catholic church received no recognition of any kind – it became, as it were, invisible to the constitution – but various prohibitions and tests were directed at those who confessed its faith. Inheritable property was restricted to Protestants. Catholics might own property but must subdivide it among their children on death. Many Catholic landowning families were to

Above The lush Boyne valley in County Meath, where James II was defeated by William of Orange in the Battle of the Boyne in 1690.

61

Right The State Ball at Dublin Castle, painted at the end of the eighteenth century by an anonymous artist. By the latter part of the eighteenth century almost all the land in Ireland was owned by the Protestant Ascendancy.

convert to Protestantism to save their estates intact; many others sank in the world as subdivision broke up the estates. There were numerous irritating or humiliating rules. A Catholic, for example, might not own a horse worth more than £5.

In spite of prolonged warfare, the Irish population had been rising in the later seventeenth century, and by 1700 amounted probably to about two million people. Three quarters or more of these were Roman Catholics, but after Limerick there was no longer any likelihood that the old Catholic ruling class — including both the ancient Gaelic families and the families descended from medieval Norman or English settlers — could command power in the land.

In Ulster there was a considerable Protestant population, apart from the "Ascendancy". This derived partly from the Plantation of nearly a century earlier, partly from the dense early-seventeenth century settlement of parts of Antrim and Down by Scottish Presbyterians, and partly from an equally important migration late in the seventeenth century.

New Protestant towns had been established in connection with the Plantation. Most of these soon came to have Catholics as well as Protestants in their population. It is common to find, in surveys of the time, "Scotch", "English" and "Irish" quarters or streets in the towns. The countryside was similarly mixed; but Ulster had acquired a character markedly different from that of the rest of the country. Already by the early eighteenth century, observers (including for example Jonathan Swift, dean of St Patrick's Cathedral in Dublin) were remarking that Ulster was the only part of Ireland that didn't look miserable and backward.

Parts of the country, mainly in the east and in the old colonial towns, had been English-speaking for centuries. English was now the language of law, government, trade and all kinds of public discourse throughout Ireland. It was the language of the new Ascendancy. It was also, although sometimes in dialect forms (including Scottish), the language of the Ulster Protestant settlement. But a large part of the Catholic population was still Irish-speaking, in parts of the east as well as most of the west.

In spite of the breakdown of their old social order, there flourished in the Irish-speaking areas of the eighteenth century a lively literature, produced by poets who no longer had the elaborate formal training of their medieval predecessors, but who composed poems in more popular forms. As the century went on, many of these turned to schoolteaching, and began providing instruction in reading, writing (in English) and arithmetic — and often much more — for the children of Catholic tenant farmers and the like. Some of the schools were in makeshift shelters, and the whole system came to be known as "hedge-schools". But when all the publicly recognized schools,

Above "The 2nd Lord Aldburgh Reviewing the Volunteers in Belan Park", painted by Francis Wheatley in 1781, is one of a series of large works commemorating the activities of the Volunteers. The Volunteers were formed by the Protestants in Ireland when Britain was fighting in America, nominally to defend Ireland while the British Army was abroad, but in effect they were the first Irish nationalists.

Left Jonathan Swift, painted here in 1718 by Charles Jervas, was the Anglican dean of St Patrick's Cathedral in Dublin and author of *Gulliver's Travels*. He wrote several pamphlets and the famous black satire *A Modest Proposal* in which he drew attention to the appalling conditions of the poor in Ireland. (National Portrait Gallery, London.)

Left Bantry Bay is on the southwest coast of Ireland. In December 1796 a huge invasion fleet of 35 French ships full of troops anchored here. They had come at the call of the United Irishmen to help bring about a republican revolution there to break the ties with England and unite the Catholics and Protestants in one Irish nation.

whether in receipt of public or of private grants, were purveyors of Protestantism as well as literacy, the hedge-schools, however makeshift, were clung to by the Catholic population as a means of acquiring education without compromising their beliefs. Some of them taught a radical dissent from both the political and the religious principles of the State, and the country schoolmaster was gradually, through changing systems and changing times, to become one of the most important transmitters of nationalist sentiments.

The Ascendancy functioned politically through its parliament in Dublin, which met more regularly in the eighteenth century than in the seventeenth. There was an implicit bargain that the Ascendancy would maintain the English interest in Ireland, while in return the British government would secure the Ascendancy's privilege. Within the scope of this broad understanding there was room for much difference of view. Attempts by the Dublin parliament to argue for its rights as the parliament of a distinct kingdom under the same crown as England were met by a Declaratory Act which asserted the subordination of the Irish parliament to Westminster. There was much friction in economic matters, mainly because of British restrictions on Irish trade. In a particularly heated dispute over a British grant of authority to a Birmingham coiner to strike coins for Ireland – which were objected to for their quality and quantity – Swift published some rousing pamphlets objecting to the British government's view of its relationship with Ireland.

Below A modern student passes the statue of George Salmon (provost of Trinity College, Dublin, from 1888 to 1904). Behind the trees are the "rubics", red brick buildings built around 1700 with Dutch gables added in the 1890s. These are the oldest surviving buildings in the College.

After the middle of the century the Irish colony began to show increasing signs of strain. There had been a very severe famine in the 1740s, causing much death and suffering in the west, but the population, though checked briefly by this, was growing. The landlords' "improvements", through enclosures, road-building and, in some cases, the introduction of new agricultural methods, contributed to social unrest, as what suited the landlords frequently disturbed their tenants. Rural secret societies began to be active, initially among Protestant tenants in the north, but soon in other parts of the country as well. The situation was eased somewhat for a while by emigration on a considerable scale. Much of this was from Ulster or the more prosperous parts of the other provinces, and it played an important part in the settlement of North America.

When the American colonies revolted, the Irish Ascendancy had very mixed feelings. They were committed to the defence of Ireland

Far Left The Customs House in Dublin, by James Gandon, was built in 1781. This beautiful building on the quays of the River Liffey was burned down during the Civil War in 1921.

Left James Gandon was also the architect of the Four Courts in Dublin, begun in 1786. This view is from the Merchant's Quay, across the River Liffey.

Above The façade of the Bank of Ireland, originally Parliament House. Begun in 1728, this was the first building in the world designed and built to house a parliament. It was sold to the Bank of Ireland after the Act of Union in 1800, and the present parliament now sits in the Dáil, Leinster House.

Right Florence Court in County Fermanagh, one of the most beautiful houses in Ulster, was built by Lord Mount Florence in 1764. It was badly damaged by fire in 1955, but has since been restored by the National Trust to its former glory.

Far Right Dunboy Castle, near Castletownberehaven in County Cork, was built in 1866 and burnt down in 1921 during the Troubles. The Civil War ended two days later.

against Britain's enemies, notably France, but they had much sympathy for the insurgent Americans, colonists whose problems and grievances in many ways resembled their own. They formed a Volunteer force to help in the defence of Irish shores, since the British needed so many soldiers for the American war; but they soon began to use the Volunteers for other purposes, including a challenge to the British government on the issue of the relationships between the two parliaments. The British, in difficulties, repealed the acts which gave offence, and the Irish legislature became independent in 1782. Although the British retained executive powers, and continued as before to "manage" as best they could the Dublin parliament – persuading it to vote most of the measures they required – the independent Irish parliament is commonly known as "Grattan's parliament", from Henry Grattan, the chief spokesman of the "patriots", or Irish, as distinct from British, interest.

The arrangement soon became, from the British point of view, dangerously unworkable. There were new problems caused by the French Revolution and a new kind of war with France – an ideological war. Many people in the British Isles had sympathy – initially at least – with the revolution and its objectives, and much political excitement was generated. Political societies of radical democratic views were formed, and became an object of concern to the government. In Ireland an organization was formed shortly after the outbreak of the French Revolution: the United Irishmen. One of its most active founder-members was Theobald Wolfe Tone, a young man of adventurous character who had developed radical and revolutionary ideas.

Such societies were formed elsewhere too, but in Ireland they soon impinged on the activities and membership of the agrarian secret societies which had been active, on and off, since soon after the middle of the century. The activities of the "Whiteboys", in Tipperary and neighboring counties, about 1760, had amounted to a virtual rebellion. In south Ulster, conflict had developed between rival Catholic and Protestant secret societies. The Catholics had a widespread organization known as the "Defenders". The Protestants, in 1795, formed the Orange Order, after a bloody affray with the Defenders. The United Irishmen, forced underground as they became more radical in their ideas, committed to a republic, drew upon the Defenders' organization to broaden their movement.

The government, through its numerous spies and informers, was well informed about these developments, and in 1797 and 1798 moved against the conspirators who planned a French Revolution in Ireland. Soldiers moved into the most dangerously disaffected areas (mostly in Ulster), searching houses, flogging and inflicting other punishments, often to the

Right A typical Georgian terrace in Dublin.

Left Following the 1798 rebellion in Ireland, Robert Emmet led a rising in Dublin in 1803 that ended more as a street riot than a rebellion. This engraving by George Cruikshank depicts the murder of Lord Kilwarden in Dublin during the insurrection.

Below Robert Emmet hid in Dublin's oldest pub, The Brazen Head, for a month while on the run before he was caught and executed. The Brazen Head is in Bridge Street near the River Liffey.

death, and generally intimidating all who might have felt inclined to show sympathy, actively or passively, to rebellion. Government agents also arrested many of the planners and organizers of insurrection. In spite of this, or, partly, because these measures goaded some people into rash action, there were scattered and uncoordinated, but formidable, uprisings in many parts of Ireland in the summer of 1798. Fighting was bloody – perhaps as many as 50,000 people died in it. But the rebellions were crushed and terrible reprisals followed.

The British government, headed by William Pitt, now decided to put into operation a system that it had already decided was the only way to cope with the Irish problem. Expending a remarkable amount of money and patronage, even by eighteenth century standards, they persuaded the Dublin parliament to vote its own extinction, and passed through the British parliament an Act of Union, which came into operation on the first day of the new century, January 1, 1801. The United Kingdom of Great Britain and Ireland came into existence. Ireland ceased to have a parliament, but from now on was to elect 100 Members of Parliament to the House of Commons in Westminster as well as contributing a number of peers and bishops to the House of Lords there.

Many members of the Protestant Ascendancy were dismayed at the loss of their colonial parliament in which, to some extent, they had been able to manage their own affairs. Members of the parliament, who shared this dismay but had been persuaded to overcome their feelings, were handsomely compensated. Many of the leaders of Catholic opinion, such as they were, were tepidly pleased with the Union, since they had been given to understand that the remaining restrictions on Catholic participation in political life would be removed after the Union. But opposition to this in Britain was too strong.

Further, the Union, in the course of a generation or two, began to appear to Protestants as the surest guarantee of their position, while Catholics had a growing sense of grievance. The pressure for parliamentary reform was changing, or threatening to change, the political balance. Numbers, majorities, counted much more than in the past. And in Ireland the already overwhelming Catholic majority appeared to be increasing, while in the United Kingdom as a whole Catholics were in a minority. The agitation for Catholic emancipation that began soon after the Union was passed was conducted initially by lobbying, which was unsuccessful. Then Daniel O'Connell, a young Catholic lawyer from a family of Kerry landowners, organized a very different kind of agitation.

He led a nationwide "Catholic Association", with two tiers of membership, to which people all over the country contributed a regular subscription in guineas or pennies. The Catholic clergy were *ex officio* members and looked after the organization at parish level. Within a few years, O'Connell presided over something uniquely new in politics, a non-violent political machine based on the mobilization of a mass

democratic movement. Through the weight of its numbers, it eventually effected the introduction of a Bill in 1829, allowing Catholics to enter Westminster parliament.

O'Connell in due course began another agitation, which was in some ways more impressive than the first, for repeal of the Act of Union. Under the Union, northeastern Ireland had developed economically and rapidly. A textile industry, based on the old linen industry but soon encompassing the manufacture of cotton cloth, was founded in the area around Lisburn and Belfast. It soon moved from home to mill production and machine manufacture, so that this part of Ireland became involved in the social and economic changes occurring in England's northeast and midlands: the "Industrial Revolution". The rest of Ireland failed to flourish this way. The country was nearly ungovernable, largely because of deficiencies both in the landholding system itself and in the social structures it supported.

The landlords remained for the most part, in the view of their tenants, alien imposters. The social cement that should have held the gentry and the other country people together with some sense of mutual obligation was very thin indeed. Absenteeism was common; subdivision of holdings and other practices made estate-management very difficult, and the evil of "rack-renting", which included penalizing the tenant for improvements, was widespread. Violence was endemic, most of it localized and concerned with matters like the bitterly resented tithe (a tax for the maintenance of the ministers of the established church) and the fees exacted from the people for the support of their own priests, as well as rent. This smoldering grievance was from time to time given a wider political meaning, and was given added weight by the rapid increase in the size of the population, which rose from about 5 million in 1800 to considerably more than 8 million in 1841 (in spite of considerable emigration to Britain and North America).

To repeal the Union in such circumstances would – so it seemed to most Protestants in particular – lead to disaster. There was very little support for the proposal in the British parliament, and an articulate opposition to it developed in Ulster. O'Connell himself

Far Left Thatched cottages abound in the green fields of Ireland. This one nestles by the sea near Derrybeg, County Donegal. This would have been the home of a poor Irish family.

Left In contrast, Mount Stewart in County Waterford, renowned for its beautiful gardens, would have housed the rich.

appeared to use the repeal agitation partly as a means of putting pressure on the government to yield more limited reforms in Ireland. For a short time it seemed that this might succeed: the agitation was muted; the government made some small attempts to meet Irish grievances; the level of violence dropped sharply. Then, with a change of administration, this process ended, and in the early 1840s O'Connell organized and led his vast army of beggars in an extraordinary political cam-

paign. He summoned and addressed enormous mass-meetings, some of them held at places (such as Tara) of great romantic and historic interest. When he announced a meeting for Clontarf, on the outskirts of Dublin, however, the government banned it and O'Connell called it off. It was difficult, without any body of support in parliament, to see where he could go from there. He himself was growing old; he was increasingly in conflict with an organization of young men – known as "Young

Below "A View of Sackville Street" (now O'Connell Street), Dublin, showing Nelson's Pillar. The colonnades of the General Post Office can be seen on the left. This painting by Michael Angelo Hayes now hangs in the National Gallery of Ireland.

Ireland"– who were romantic nationalists, originally his supporters but with views growing increasingly different from his. They romanticized war and violence and they thought he catered too much to Catholic, rather than secular Irish or national interests.

All this was overtaken by the major disaster of the 1840s, remembered in Ireland, because of its scale, as "the Famine" (although there had been other famines). Blight destroyed the potato-crop, the food on which more than half the population lived. It appeared widely in 1845 and everywhere in 1846. In 1847, seed-potatoes had not been sown. Tens of thousands of people starved to death. The hunger was followed by epidemics of disease, which claimed more hundreds of thousands of lives. Dreadful scenes were witnessed, especially in the overcrowded squatters' potato-patches in the west of Ireland. After the famine there was a great tide of emigration, almost all to North America, that was to go on for years. The

Below Dingle peninsula in County Kerry.

Bottom Two brightly painted doors in a Georgian terrace in Dublin. Doors of this type may be found all over Dublin, and often have intricate fanlights above.

Below The failure of the potato crop and the resulting Famine of 1845-9 left thousands of Irish people starving and homeless. Those who had gave: in this engraving a girl distributes clothing to the poor from the back of a cart at Kilrush, County Clare.

population fell sharply and went on falling for the rest of the century.

The government was hampered in its handling of this calamity both by the inadequacy of its administrative machinery, and, much more, by the prevailing preconceived ideas on political economy. A reluctance to interfere or compete with market forces resulted in no direct government intervention, except when it came to be too late for many of the starving people. The emigrants carried overseas with them a hatred of British rule (which they blamed) that was to persist for generations.

In the wake of the famine some of the Young Irelanders attempted to improvise an uprising, which was a total failure but which helped to

commit a section of Irish political opinion, opposed to the Union, to conspiratorial organization and the use of armed force. Within another generation, a more formidable organization on such lines was created – the Fenians – whose Irish Republican Brotherhood, sworn to the achievement of an independent Irish republic, was to persist into the twentieth century as a small but stubborn body, with the potential for re-establishing a large-scale organization. The Fenians too attempted an uprising, in 1867, which again came to nothing.

But a different kind of revolution took place in the later nineteenth century, as the result of the conjunction of several powerful forces. One was the political organization of masses of people, such as had been pioneered by O'Connell. An agitation for "home rule"– that is, for an assembly in Ireland with some limited powers of government in purely Irish affairs, came under the leadership of a County Wicklow landlord, Charles Stewart Parnell, who succeeded in bringing a group of Irish MPs at Westminster under tight party discipline and fighting within the House of Commons itself,

as well as on the hustings, a political campaign that made full use of the Irish advantage (when they had it) of holding the balance of power between Liberals and Conservatives. These tactics were successful to the extent that two Home Rule bills were introduced, in 1886 and in 1893. Although both were defeated (in different ways) Home Rule had become a central issue in British politics and was to continue so.

Another force, partly marshaled by the same Parnell, partly by others, such as Michael Davitt, was the agrarian grievance that had smoldered in violence for two centuries. Organization on a national scale, working together with political agitation and parliamentary activity, led to a series of government concessions, in the form of land purchase and other land bills. By the beginning of the twentieth century a great social revolution was in progress: transfer of land

Above Those who could, escaped the Famine by emigrating, many to America. This group wait on the quay, surrounded by their belongings, for a boat to take them to a new life on the other side of the Atlantic.

Above Charles Stewart Parnell, painted in 1892 by Sydney Hall. An Irish Protestant landlord, Parnell dominated British parliamentary life in the 1880s. In ten brief years he raised Irish national feeling in his demand for Irish Home Rule, before his involvement in a divorce scandal brought his career to an abrupt end. (National Gallery of Ireland.)

from the landowners to their tenants, under government pressure and supervision.

The third force was that of the Fenians and their successors: armed conspiracy to overthrow the British State in Ireland. This remained in the background while the revolution in land ownership was accomplished; but its background presence played some part in the events of this time.

Home Rule was defeated in the nineteenth century with the aid of industrialized Protestant Ulster which had undergone a divergent development. It was also checked by the personal tragedy of Parnell, the result of his involvement in a divorce case. Gladstone, the British Liberal Prime Minister with whom he had worked, called on the Irish party to rid itself of a leader who was morally unacceptable. Parnell refused to go, the party split, with the Catholic church joining with Parnell's opponents. Then he died, leaving an atmosphere of bitterness that caused many young people to turn from "politics".

They turned instead to cultural matters: the revival and organization of traditional Irish games; the study and attempted revival of the

Irish language; the development of ideas of an "Irish Ireland". This turning aside was to prove in the long run to be far more potent politics than "politics".

Liam de Paor

Left In the late 1870s a second famine threatened, and again families unable to pay the rent were evicted from their homes. This pitiful photograph was taken in County Fermanagh in the 1880s.

Above Michael Davitt, MP, agitated for reduction of rents and an end to evictions. He and Parnell launched the Land League together. This portrait of Davitt was painted by William Orpen and now hangs in the Municipal Gallery, Dublin.

The Twentieth Century

4

In 1902 Dublin was stirred into controversy by the first performance of a play by the poet William Butler Yeats. *Cathleen ni Houlihan* summoned Ireland's young men to the ancient cause of rebellion against the foreign usurper. In a moment of brilliant theatricality before the final curtain, the little old woman who has mysteriously visited a peasant cottage to issue this summons is transformed into a beautiful young girl with "the walk of a queen".

One man who saw the performance thought that such plays should not be produced "unless one was prepared for people to go out to shoot and be shot". The actress who played the part of the little old woman was Maud Gonne, whom a contemporary newspaper described as "the well-known political agitator". A famed beauty, she was the unattainable object of Yeats's undying ardor, a fanatically committed nationalist and the daughter of an English army officer. In her own person she embodied many of the contradictions and complexities of Ireland in the twentieth century. Half English, appearing in a play by an Irish Protestant, fomenting a rebellion that would threaten her own class, she managed in a moment of magnificent gesture to catch the imagination of a nation. For the image of Ireland as simultaneously young and old, as subject to an ancient tyranny but with her essential beauty still fresh, is the basis of much of the country's national feeling.

Indeed it was the image of Cathleen ni Houlihan that was to work on the imagination of a generation of poets, theorists and dreamers who recklessly declared the Republic of Ireland at the Post Office during the Easter of 1916. Cathleen ni Houlihan's image – and that of Cuchulainn, the heroic figure from the mythological past whom Yeats had brought to life in poem and play. Their noble and doomed act of defiance had much of the theatrical about it. The stage this time was history and the players, who in their individual lives embodied perhaps as many contradictions as had Maud Gonne (Patrick Pearse himself who read the Proclamation on the steps of the Post Office was son to an English father), were caught up in an heroic gesture which in Yeats's famous words expressed the "terrible beauty" of a nation's destiny.

The compelling purity of such moments cannot, of course, be sustained. The years of guerilla warfare that the gesture of 1916 stimulated and the sad squalor of the Civil War which followed the Treaty with Great Britain in 1922 (which allowed 26 counties of Ireland something akin to Dominion status) forced that truth home. The service of Cathleen was a cruel one, her moods and whims treacherous. Yet, in developing the arts of modern guerilla warfare in those years, the Irish were not only bravely demonstrating to the world the power of ancestral feelings but offering an object lesson in the hard school of twentieth-century

Left The ruins of the General Post Office in Sackville Street (now O'Connell Street), Dublin, after the Easter Rising of 1916. The photograph was taken from Nelson's Pillar which was itself blown up in 1966.

Below Maud Gonne, famed beauty, talented actress, and "political agitator".

anti-imperial struggle – a lesson which was to be soundly learned in many parts of the world.

When the dust had settled it was possible to see what the years of blood had effected. Ireland was partitioned into two administrative areas. In one, Northern Ireland, a local parliament exercising powers devolved from Westminster protected the political and social interests of the Protestant majority of six northern counties; in the other, a new government slowly took control of 26 county states in which the great majority of citizens were in fact conservatively minded rural dwellers loyal to an austere and authoritarian Catholicism. A national revolution had taken place – the Union Jack no longer flew over Dublin Castle – but the social order in both parts of the island had not been radically disturbed. The new government in the Irish Free State, as it was known, essentially represented the interests of the landowners of rural Ireland, that class whose power had been asserted in the late nineteenth century and which had seized control of their farms from Anglo-Irish landlords through a series of Land Acts of the Westminster parliament.

It was Anglo-Ireland which was the principal victim of the national revolution. That once aggressively powerful social caste, identified by political support of the union with Great Britain, by Protestantism of the Anglican variety, by possession of vast tracts of the Irish soil and by patrician disdain for the mass of the Irish people, endured an eclipse as rapid and total in the early twentieth century as that of Tsarist Russia. Many of their sons perished in the Great War, many great families chose exile when it was clear Irish independence was inevitable and many of their Big Houses were razed to the ground in the fires of the War of Independence and the Civil War. Between 1921 and 1923 at least 192 such houses met this fate.

For Ireland the destruction of these houses was a real loss. They contained many fine pictures, much good Irish furniture and they had been designed and built by Irish craftsmen and workers. It has been only in recent years that modern Ireland has begun to recognize this fact and has sought to preserve those examples of Anglo-Ireland's architecture that escaped the fires of war and the effects of protracted neglect.

Fortunately, much of Anglo-Ireland's legacy to modern Ireland took less perishable form. For, as their class had lost its political and

Below The ruthless Black and Tans, dressed in distinctive khaki, search a GPO waggon in Dublin in 1920.

Left Egerton Sheswel-White, owner of Bantry House, in the Rose Room with its Gobelin tapestries. Built in 1771, Bantry survived the Troubles, but maintenance is a never-ending problem.

Above The eighteenth-century Doneraile Court is now being restored by the Georgian Society.

Right The annual Trinity Ball is an occasion for celebration at Trinity College, Dublin, which remains a particularly Anglo-Irish institution.

Below "The Plough and the Stars" by Sean O'Casey caused riots when first performed at the Abbey Theatre in 1926, because of its unheroic treatment of the 1916 Rising.

social power, a number of enlightened and brilliantly creative individuals, associated in varying ways with Anglo-Ireland, had committed themselves to the cultural renewal of their country. Douglas Hyde, son of a Church of Ireland clergyman, who was later to become Ireland's first President, had helped to found the Gaelic League which strove energetically to revive the vernacular use of Ireland's ancient tongue. Lady Gregory of Coole in County Galway and W. B. Yeats established the Abbey Theatre, which in 1925 was to receive a state subsidy from the new government (the first theater in the world to receive patronage of this kind); and Yeats himself was to bring honor on the new State, of whose parliament he was a Senator, when in 1923 he received the Nobel Prize for Literature. The poet's sure aesthetic sense made itself felt in the very practical matter of money: he served on the committee which decided upon the quite beautiful designs for an Irish coinage.

Distinctive Anglo-Irish institutions survived in the new state – the Royal Irish Academy (with its traditions of learning and scholarship), Trinity College, Dublin (one of the oldest universities in the English-speaking world) and the Royal Dublin Society, which at its annual Horse Show in the capital allowed a new political and social elite to mix with their former masters in an atmosphere of relaxed style and shared enthusiasm for thoroughbred horse flesh. Anglo-Ireland's experience in this century of bitter anti-colonialism was markedly fortunate – the fact that Dublin's two cathedrals remain to this day centers of Anglican worship reflects a profound tolerance at the heart of Irish life. But something of Anglo-Ireland's sense of social disintegration and loss was expressed in the work of Ireland's other Nobel Laureate for Literature, Samuel Beckett, who made his own anguished response to a Protestant upbringing in a stiflingly genteel Dublin suburb of the 1920s a metaphor for the spiritual dislocation of modern man.

The new state was not all tolerance, however. An Irish identity had to be forged and protected. The Irish language was to be revived, Catholic values imposed in crucial areas of personal morality (divorce, for example, was forbidden). A rigorous censorship of literature was established in 1929 which for almost four decades was to ban works by almost every twentieth century writer of note. Church and state seemed united in a crusade to maintain a *cordon sanitaire* around the country. A

Bottom Sniper and lookouts in a Dublin street during the Civil War of 1922 which was precipitated by the Anglo-Irish Treaty of 1921.

Below W. B. Yeats, the poet, Sligo's most famous son and a Nobel Prizewinner (1865-1939).

conservative people was governed by conservative politicians who deferred to priest and prelate. Of priests there was no shortage. Religion was a growth industry flourishing in a society where droves of young people emigrated each year from a country in which they could find no livelihood. And they left to a chorus of ecclesiastical warnings on the temptations they would face in pagan England, America and Australia and with denunciations of the dangers of sexual license ringing in their ears. Reasons for the extraordinary puritanism of newly independent Ireland are not hard to come by: the economic rigors of life on the small farms throughout the country enforced sexual abstinence where a premarital pregnancy could be ruinous; an insecure nationalism encouraged zealous excess, an isolationism of manners and morals.

But it is hard not to sense something older, more rooted in perennial aspects of the Irish psyche which link modern pilgrimages still undertaken by large numbers to such holy sites as Lough Derg and Croagh Patrick with the ancient ascetism of Celtic Christianity.

From 1932 onwards (with brief interruptions) the austere, distinctly clerical Eamon de Valera presided over this inward-looking society

Far Left A farmer shears sheep on a lonely hill farm in Kerry watched by his sister.

Left A disused railway station outside Derry serves as a reminder of more affluent Victorian days.

Left Herding the cows along a road in Connemara.

of cautious shopkeepers, farmers and small businessmen, a society one disenchanted writer bitterly satirized as "the Grocers' Republic". De Valera aspired to Irish self-sufficiency. Neutrality in the Second World War was an expression of his dedication to the absolute of national independence. What he wanted for his people was, as he told them on St Patrick's Day in 1943, an Ireland:

which we dreamed . . . would be the home of a people who valued material wealth only as a basis of right living, of a people who were satisfied with frugal comfort and devoted their leisure to the things of the spirit; a land whose countryside would be bright with cosy homesteads, whose fields and villages would be joyous with sounds of industry, the romping of sturdy

children, the contests of athletic youths, the laughter of comely maidens; whose firesides would be the forums of the wisdom of serene old age.

Such a romantic view of Irish life, though commendable for its idealism, took little account of the desperate poverty of much of rural and urban Ireland, of an emigration that was draining the country of its energetic young and of the human waste which an angry, eloquent poet exposed in his terrifying long poem of 1942, *The Great Hunger*. Patrick Kavanagh's work indeed was an indictment of a political and social order which delivered to so many only a living death. Cathleen ni Houlihan had surrendered to a possessive widowed mother who demanded no sacrifice of her sons on the altar of patriotism. She sought

Far Left A typical brightly-painted Irish shop front complete with thatched roof in "the Grocers' Republic".

Above Supping a pint in the town of Kinvara, County Galway.

Left Eamon de Valera inaugurated as President of the Republic of Ireland.

from them rather the lifelong self-abnegation of sexual abstinence.

The Irish Free State was founded in 1922. The same year James Joyce published his major novel, *Ulysses*. The Free State seemed dedicated to an image of Ireland as uniquely pious and self-sufficient. Joyce's great book, immortalizing Dublin as few other novels have done for any other place, revealed by contrast that Irish people were much the same as people the world over. Rich in local, distinguishing characteristics of wit, love of myth, gossip and song, they nevertheless share with most of humanity a taste for the drink and normally various sexual needs. Molly Bloom, whose ripe soliloquy concludes the book, is no better than she should be, and all the better for that, as representative of Irish womanhood. She gave the lie to all who wanted to pretend that the Ireland of Cathleen ni Houlihan and the possessive mother was the only one.

By the 1950s Ireland's economic and social problems had become acute. The quest for self-sufficiency was obviously futile in a decade when emigration and unemployment were putting in question the very existence of the state. It was time for a new departure. Under the energetic leadership of a new prime minister, Sean Lemass, Ireland took the decision to abandon economic isolation, decided to open its economy to large-scale foreign investment. Sights were now set on European Economic Community (EEC) membership and on the consumer society. It was time to abandon dreams of a glorious past and to unleash some youthful energy. The people responded with a will. Change was the tonic. From Saskatoon to Sydney the 1960s were quickening the pace of things. Ireland was eager to join the dance. The Second Vatican Council had given Irish Catholicism a less intimidating face; the national television station which began broadcasting in 1962 opened the air-waves to vigorous debates on traditional values. Hemlines went up, inhibitions down. Fortunes. were being made.

In 20 years the young Republic (which had been formally declared in 1949) underwent a social transformation. Emigration ceased almost completely, the population which had

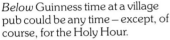

Below Guinness time at a village pub could be any time – except, of course, for the Holy Hour.

Left The puck sits between the Republican Tricolour and the Ulster flag during the Annual Puck Fair in Killorglin, County Kerry.

Below Sean Lemass (left) and the Chairman of Irish Sugar inspect crops growing on reclaimed bogland. As Prime Minister, Sean Lemass greatly improved the Irish economy.

91

declined inexorably since the famine of the 1840s began to climb (it now stands at three and a quarter million). A society that had been marked by the preponderance of elderly and unmarried people became unique in western Europe for the youthfulness and fertility of its citizenry. By the end of the 1970s over half the population was under 25 years of age. Education not religion was now the boom industry giving contemporary Ireland one of the best educated populations in the world.

In the 1960s and 1970s Ireland changed from a rural to an urban society. Dublin's population grew to over a million while the flight from the small farms of rural Ireland left much of the countryside in the hands of new-style entrepreneurial farmers who exploited the agricultural policies of the EEC (Ireland entered in 1973) to remarkable effect. A landscape that had scarcely changed since the nineteenth century produced, in the 1970s, a crop of luxurious bungalows, banishing the traditional cottage to the tourist brochure and the exile's dream.

The strain on the burgeoning cities was enormous, Dublin particularly bearing the brunt. Huge new housing developments sprang up where thousands of young families, many of them recently uprooted from the land, tried to cope with the demands of urban life. Often basic services were neglected in these new wastelands and "alienation" entered the vocabulary of Irish ills. But foreign holidays

Below This *trompe l'oeil* bungalow at Ballybunion, County Kerry, is a far cry from the traditional Irish cottage at Ballyness Bay, County Donegal *(Far Left)*.

were cheap, the Costa del Sol a yearly parole from commuter bus and supermarket lineup. And things were getting better. Weren't they?

Well, yes and no. Certainly there was a genuine rise in living standards (between 1957 and 1980 there was an 80 per cent rise in personal consumption per head in real terms and disposable personal income in real terms doubled in the same period). But such statistics disguise what studies of Irish poverty in the 1970s suggested: that at least a quarter of the population and perhaps one third lived below a "poverty-line" estimated on the basis of social security levels of payment. And the burden of foreign debt increased rapidly in the same decade to provoke serious economic crises in the 1980s. And there was the appalling, threatening problem of the north.

Since 1922 all Irish governments had been dedicated to the anti-partition cause. The border was a wound inflicted on the Irish nation by the duplicitous Lloyd George. Only its removal would end the old quarrel with England. The fact that a million Protestant Unionists were implacably opposed to incorporation in an all-Ireland state was to a very

Below For some, the standard of life is improving, but for others it continues below the poverty line.

great extent simply ignored. It was naïvely assumed that, when the British decided to leave Ireland, the Unionists would come to their senses and throw in their lot with the island's majority. In expectation of that utopian outcome, nothing much was done for 40 years to make reunification any kind of practical possibility. Indeed, a state intent on enshrining Catholic social policy in its legislation and Constitution and on emphasizing the Gaelic traditions of its people might well be considered to have consolidated partition itself. Furthermore a state which could not provide its own population with a decent standard of living could hardly lay serious claims on an economically better placed population in a neighboring jurisdiction. It was Sean Lemass, a practical visionary, who saw that reunification could only occur when the Republic had achieved sufficient economic power to make it possible and that, in the meantime, the two parts of Ireland should co-operate to their mutual advantage. On an historic day in January 1965 Lemass visited the Prime Minister of Northern Ireland at the Stormont Parliament Buildings in Belfast. Perhaps north and

Below Cobh, County Cork, the bustling cheerful harbor for Cork City with the omnipresent church towering over it.

95

Right Ian Paisley (not Reverend) leads a Loyalist rally at Belfast City Hall. The slogan "No surrender" survives from the Siege of Derry.

Above The presence of the British Army (seen here on the streets of Newry) is reassuring to some and provoking to others.

south could, in pursuit of realistic aims, break the log-jam of decades of suspicion and prejudice and in eventual EEC membership make the border an anachronistic irrelevance. It was not to be.

Terence O'Neill, the Northern Irish Prime Minister, had announced in 1964 that he intended "to make Northern Ireland prosperous and to build bridges between the two traditions in our community". This and his meeting with Lemass and a later visit to Dublin itself were too much for some of his Northern Irish enemies. The ambitious, demagogic Ian Paisley exploited fears of a sellout by O'Neill to revive old sectarian passions upon whose back he hoped to rise to power. There could be no accommodation with Irish nationalism nor any compromise with the Catholic nationalist minority in the Northern state. They had never accepted the validity of partition and treacherously withheld loyalty from Queen and country. Such was Paisley's poisonous message. No surrender.

The Catholic minority in Northern Ireland had endured four decades of second class citizenship and discrimination. A new generation of educated young people in its midst, which had seized the educational opportunities afforded by the British Welfare State, was quite unprepared to accept that Northern Catholics should continue to be so abused by the resented majority. The Civil Rights movement was born, bred of the radicalism of young people everywhere in the 1960s and of a profound sense of social and national grievance. Reaction from the majority was swift and bloody. Civil disruption quickly went beyond the control of the local forces of law and order and the British Army was dispatched by the British Government to restore and maintain the peace. And there they have remained since 1969, through 16 years of the violence that has made Belfast and Derry on a par with Saigon, Teheran and Beirut as objects of the

Below The women's peace movement was started by Mairead Corrigan and Betty Williams after many years of violence in Northern Ireland. They were awarded the Nobel Peace Prize in 1976.

international media's sporadic attention.

In the 1960s the Irish Republican Army had seemed a defeated force. This small group of guerillas (illegal in both parts of Ireland), dedicated to the removal of the border and to Irish unity, had called off a military campaign in 1962 when failure stared it in the face. In the era of O'Neill and Lemass, of consumerism and ecumenism, it had seemed irrelevant, part of the past. The civil disturbances of the late 1960s in Northern Ireland, and the presence on the streets in Derry and Belfast of the old enemy, the British Army, once more gave the guerilla a sea in which to swim. Nurtured in the Catholic ghetto's fear of sectarian attack and anger at the heavy-handed excesses of the British soldiery, the provisional IRA emerged in the early 1970s as a well-organized determined guerilla army which has sustained its campaign of warfare in Northern Ireland and Britain ever since.

In comparison with guerilla wars in other parts of the world, "the troubles" in the north might seem a tame affair. In many areas of the province, life has continued almost normally. The IRA exercises, despite the propaganda, a certain restraint, as does the British Army. Horrific atrocities have been committed by all sides, but periods of comparative peace allow the underlying problems of the area to seem less in need of immediate attention than they are. The IRA and the British Army have each achieved a kind of stalemate in which neither can defeat the other. Life goes on. And so does the war.

But Northern Ireland is a small place, about the size of Yorkshire. Its population of one and a half million lives mostly in the Belfast and Derry areas where the violence has been most spectacular. So war has become an intimate part of the people's consciousness. Everyone knows someone who has been killed or injured. A weirdly local, almost domestic, war is how ordinary people experience it. Gelignite mixed in with the soup spoons. Blood on the kitchen floor. And an entire generation has grown up in

Below A Loyalist mural in Coleraine, County Derry, celebrates the victory of King Billy (William of Orange) at the Battle of the Boyne in 1690.

Left Industrial Belfast.

Below This Sinn Fein mural on the Falls Road, west Belfast, looks forward to a better future.

the ghettos for whom checkpoints, summary arrest and interrogation, the sniper's bullet, are taken for normality.

Reactions in the south to the Northern trauma have been various. A small minority has given active support and encouragement to the IRA, providing safe houses to men on the run, passing on information. An indeterminate, though probably not large, section of the population gives tacit support to the movement while regretting some of its methods. Most people just hope "the troubles" can be contained north of the border and try to ignore them. On two occasions it seemed that would be impossible. In 1972, following Bloody Sunday in Derry when British paratroopers shot dead 13 unarmed civil rights marchers, a wave of popular revulsion led to the burning of the British Embassy in Dublin and to a sense that national honor might demand even greater retribution. Almost ten years later the deaths of ten republican hunger strikers in a Northern jail revived atavistic feelings that threatened to overwhelm the official moderation which has governed the Irish state's response to the Northern crisis throughout. At these moments it was as if Cathleen ni Houlihan was once again challenging the nation with her message of blood and sacrifice.

Two things may account for the fact that this message has lacked its former mesmeric power. Nightly television reports have brought home to most people the sheer ghastliness of modern terrorist violence, the difference, in John Synge's words, between "a gallous story" and "a dirty deed". And a taste of prosperity has made many disinclined to exchange a recently achieved well-being for the rigors of a war of national liberation. In recent years too, that novel Irish experience of economic success has begun to seem a temporary alleviation of the more authentic Irish condition of poverty. In times of great economic insecurity, therefore, few have much interest in further rocking the ship of state in waters that are already so turbulent.

The Irish economy after two decades of buoyancy is now in deep recession. The worldwide economic depression of the 1980s has bitten deeper in Ireland than in most places. Foreign indebtedness is disastrously high, unemployment at unparalleled levels; the taxation burden is severe with a large public sector and many dependent people placing heavy demands on the state. Youth unemployment is a particularly grievous problem. Crime rates in the capital have risen dramatically; vandalism and drug-trafficking seem endemic. Farmers, after a decade of expansion and profit, have had to cope with falling prices and the problems of over-production in the EEC. In Cork, the departure of the Ford motor company which had maintained a plant in the city since the 1920s indicated how risky was the state's dependence on multinational investment. Businesses go bankrupt as a black economy burgeons. In the west of the country in recent months old people have been attacked in their homes by roving gangs intent on their meager savings – an appalling symptom of acute social malaise.

Yet the success of the 1960s and 1970s still sustains the Irish in their belief in themselves as does the very existence of their state, forged by their own efforts after centuries of subjugation and colonial mismanagement. Pride and national conviction, a developing determination to solve the Northern question, are elements in a spirit of resolution which, despite the odds, keeps public life healthy, the people in good heart. Patriotism, in other words, rules OK. Not the narrow nationalism of the fanatics, nor the complacent superiority of the

Below St Patrick's Quay, Cork.

Right The IRA funeral of hunger striker Joe McDonnell was marked in true fashion by a gun salute. The gunmen are masked and the coffin is draped in the Irish Tricolour.

Left Drug trafficking has recently become a major problem in Dublin. Here, concerned parents demonstrate against drug pushers.

ex-colonial powers, but a pleasure in Irish achievement at home and abroad. The wealth of Irish America, now the second most prosperous ethnic group in the United States, is a source of gratification but so is the work of Irish missionaries in the developing world, as is the generosity of Irish response to African famine. The role of Irish forces in UN peacekeeping expresses a sense of international responsibility, a concern to participate as a voice of reason in the world. The popularity of Irish writers abroad, the invasion of the British media by skilled Irish communicators, gives much satisfaction. A George Best or a Barry McGuigan unites north and south as little else can. A James Galway gives us all a lift. The country still feels young, at the start of something, its vibrantly youthful population unprepared to accept the shibboleths and catch-phrases of the past. But it remains a country aware of an inheritance of music, language, literature and sports bequeathed to it from a troubled but rich antiquity.

And it remains hauntingly beautiful.

Terence Brown

Below Leinster House, Dublin, the seat of Irish Government (the Dáil).

102

Overleaf This wildlife sanctuary is near Courtmascherry in County Cork.

Left A John F. Kennedy tapestry in Krugers Bar, Dunguin, County Kerry. After Kennedy's assassination, mourning Irish people hung pictures of this most famous Irish American beside those of the Virgin Mary.

Below Garret FitzGerald and Charlie Haughey, side by side, silently convince the electorate of County Meath.

The Irish:
Priests and the People

or some curious and incurious reasons, almost every Irish person has a deep interest in religion, even, or perhaps especially, when he declares himself agnostic or atheist. The statistic most often slung about states that "96 per cent of the people of the Republic are Catholics". An Irish Catholic is not always easily identifiable as a Christian, and in Ireland that is the real problem. You are expected to be a Catholic but being a Christian is quite a different matter. As a result of this situation, this spiritual statistic, Ireland is full of Catholics but a little short on Christians. The possibility that one may be both does not strike too many people. Christians are strangely Protestant.

An interesting fact is that very few Irish people know much about the Bible. It's a Protestant book. There *is*, mind you, a Catholic version called the Douai Bible; but it is rhetorical and sloppy and elaborately imprecise, a badly written thing. Good Irish Catholics know next to nothing about the Bible. That is a book for "the other side".

That phrase "the other side" says a great deal about religion in Ireland. Religion should unite people in love. In Ireland, it frequently divides them in hatred and violence. The chief reason for this sad state of division, I think, is that many Irish people are saturated in religion from early childhood. Subsequently, what should be religious belief becomes religious prejudice. What should be religious tolerance too often becomes religious animosity.

When I was a child, we used to have exams in Religious Knowledge. The Albigensian Heresy and the like. (Important influences on Kerry football!) For about six or seven weeks each year, we studied nothing all day and all

Left Rosaries and religious pictures, such as this one of the last supper, are decorations frequently found in Irish Catholic houses.

Below The Pope celebrates open air Mass in Derry during his visit to Ireland in 1979.

night long but this thing called Religious Knowledge. We ate, drank, slept and dreamed it. At the end of that time there was an exam. There we were, in the heart of Kerry, or as close to it as makes no difference, scribbling away about the Albigensian Heresy and Martin Luther and that scamp Calvin and the Reformation and the Holy Trinity and the concept of Transubstantiation and other simple matters like that. In the school I attended, there was a hilly field where we played football and chatted about the Albigensian Heresy and the Virgin Birth and Three-Persons-In-One and how we would all be looking at each other on the day of the Resurrection. There was one fellow, "the Scratcher" Roche, greatly given to self-examination of an arduous physical kind, who said he would buy a comb for the Resurrection. Between you and me, that was a fair idea. "The Scratcher" Roche was inordinately scruffy, as bad as myself, in fact. Any man should be well combed for the Resurrection.

This Religious Knowledge got into our hearts and minds and blood and bones. In Ireland, religion is an assault on consciousness. It is not sporadic; it is pervasive and permanent. It takes you over. It is a form of spiritual imperialism. It dominates your ways of thinking and feeling. It invests you with images that cannot be forgotten. You cannot flirt with Catholicism. It is a love-affair or a hate-affair. Either way, it invades the soul. People often think they can shake it off. They cannot. Not completely, anyway. Irish Catholicism is sometimes said to be mindless, simply because there is no strong tradition of individual thinking among Irish theologians. But that is precisely its strength. There are no individual Irish theologians of any consequence. That would be dangerous. The slogan of an Irish theologian could well be, "I do not think; therefore I am". There is a kind of collective anonymous strength, reflected in those urbane meetings of Bishops in Maynooth. Individualism is obviously frowned on. "We're there together, lads. We'll steer the old ship together as a well-organized crew and no-one will know who the captain is. Ah, sure, the captain is in Rome. If none of us is prominent, we can all pretend to be evident".

The most amazing thing of all, actually, is that in spite of what I have said, Irish Catholicism is far removed from Roman Catholicism. This is so, I believe, because Ireland is an island washed by a sea of prejudice, an island careful to guard its own ways of looking at life, mindful of its own inherited values, consciously apart from Europe though uneasily allied to it,

Right An old woman of Aran, wearing the traditional red petticoat, watches the arrival of a ferry.

Below Bishops have tea at St Patrick's College, Maynooth. St Patrick's was founded by the English in 1795 "for the education of people of the popish persuasion". Today, it is the site of a national seminary and a meeting place for bishops.

somewhat unknown yet proud of that very fact, sturdily independent of everything and everybody, forever looking at its own navel, happily incestuous and resolutely feckless.

What I am talking about is a deep, implacable sense of insular identity.

We are not just Irishmen. We are islandmen.

That is why Ireland is often called "quaint" or "charming" or, better still, "a delightful place to visit". These are simply ways of dismissing the extremely complex phenomenon of insularity, that state of egotistical isolation in which anything can happen.

> Out of Ireland have we come
> Great hatred, little room
> Maimed us at the start.
> I carry from my mother's womb
> A fanatic heart.

Isolated fanaticism. A state of severed intensity. Pleasant decent people so riddled with prejudice it will amaze you to witness it once you touch it. (I am quite sure this article I am writing is full of prejudices that I cannot even recognize. That is the nature of prejudice: you are so full of it you cannot even see it. Yet let me not be intimidated by this recognition!)

Left The new generation of Ireland: children play in the streets as their parents did before them.

Below Religion is present in all aspects of Irish life. These fishing boats in Howth are being blessed to ensure good fishing.

The Irish Catholic Church is full of this kind of prejudice. The nuns are only ornaments, bright and beautiful as many of them are. The bishops and priests rule the roost. They want it that way. They smile and dominate, dominate and smile. They cut out the women. The Church is utterly sexless. It fears sex. The bishops say that it is all right to *be* sexual. But don't *do* it. Part of the tragic inadequacy of the Irish Catholic Church is that it always separates *being* from *doing.*

The true meaning of sexuality is also negated in homosexual acts and sexual relations between homosexuals. We must distinguish homosexual orientation from homosexual acts. Objectively, homosexual acts are intrinsically and gravely immoral.

Homosexual tendencies, however, as distinct from homosexual actions, can be innate and irreversible. They can cause drives and temptations which are difficult

Below Ceremonial religion: the installation of Brendan Commiskey as Bishop of Ferns at St Aidan's Cathedral in Enniscorthy, County Wexford.

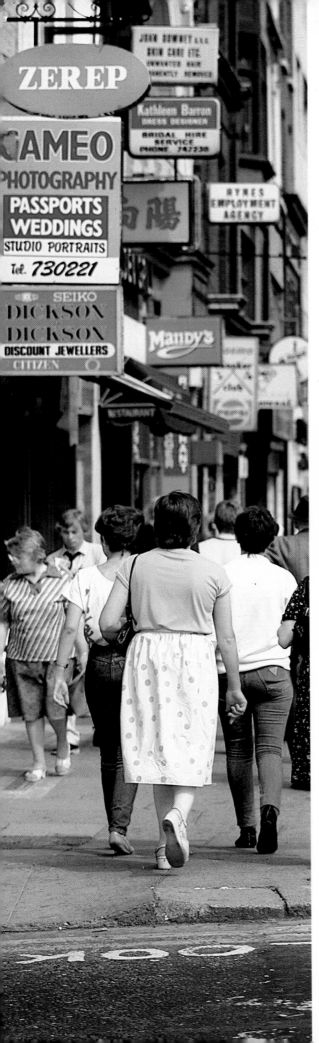

to control or resist. For such persons, some homosexual actions may well lack the full freedom and deliberateness necessary to constitute grave sin. Each case must be judged individually and compassionately.

I can sense two things from that piece of writing in the Irish Bishops' Pastoral, *Love Is For Life*, 1985 (Popular Edition). Firstly, there is the preposterous situation in which a collection of aged, cloistered celibates tell other men how to behave with each other. (You would swear to God they knew something about what they were talking about. Some Frenchman sensibly said that of the various forms of sexual perversion, celibacy is the worst.) Secondly, there is an underlying, almost reluctant element of compassionate understanding. This is the element the bishops should develop. Go easy on the judgment. Develop the understanding. Judgment is easy, but it is always more difficult to understand what we have not

Left Two nuns in modern habits stroll down O'Connell Street in Dublin. For most of their lives they have probably been wearing habits that reached the floor.

experienced. It is arguable that a bishop pontificating about sex is like a dedicated non-drinker telling you about the qualities of various brands of Scotch whisky.

This judgmental maleness, stern and unbending and sadly convinced of its own rightness, has ensured that the rulers of the Church in Ireland are, as they have been for so long now, more interested in telling you what is wrong than what is right, more interested in respectability than in respect.

This is also why they are not very close to the people they claim to represent, the people they do, in fact, represent. These strong, intelligent, respectable bishopmen are basically more interested in power than in love. That is why they outlaw sex; except, of course, in marriage.

Above The two sides of Irish life are brought together in a shop window.

Right On the last Sunday in July, Garland Sunday, thousands of pilgrims climb laboriously to the top of Croagh Patrick in County Mayo. Many climb in bare feet in respect for St Patrick who fasted on the mountain for the 40 days of Lent in 441 AD. Autographed photographs of the Saint are sometimes for sale at the top!

Above Enniscorthy Natural Family Planners protest during a pro-life march in Dublin in January, 1983.

Marriage. I asked two Irishwomen, "What is marriage?"

The first answered, "Tryin' not to hate the man you believe you love". The second said, "It's a woman sharin' problems and troubles with a man so that she won't feel too alone". There is more wisdom in one harassed woman than in a thousand pampered bishops. But Irish bishops know all about marriage; that's why they never get married. Cute boyos.

Marriage is the taming of sex. Marriage is children, that is, the continuity and expansion of the Church. Marriage, above all, is settling a man down. Let him grow for a while; then settle him down.

It is important to grasp this idea of the implacable maleness of the Irish Catholic Church. Without it, you will not understand how they use women while pretending to put them on pedestals. One of the most effective ways to get rid of a woman is to put her on a pedestal. The notion of a Miss World is an exercise in this sort of degradation. The Irish Mother, as created by the Irish Church, is a sort of claustrophobic domestic equivalent of Miss World. Elected and vaguely idiotic, but worth adoring.

By putting women on pedestals, by turning Irishwomen into docile provincial versions of the Mother of God, the Church in Ireland, the entire male-infested institution, has used women to further and establish its own power. If a man can harness a woman's sexuality, he will guarantee his own powerful position.

Below A shrine to the Virgin under the Paps at Gortnagane, County Kerry.

There is a brief, shocking poem by Austin Clarke which illustrates this. It is about a woman going to confession to a Redemptorist. She is a woman of faith. She believes. She even believes the Redemptorist. His "advice" to obey her husband against the warning of her doctor results in a seventh and fatal pregnancy. His advice kills her.

Is he therefore a killer? How many priests have murderously advised women like this? And yet the priests believe that they themselves are "good"? What is this "goodness"? What do these priests know about women? How can they "advise" them? This particular priest has no hesitation in telling this particular woman what to do. Obey your husband or be damned. This is the maleness of the Irish Church at its most authoritative, advisory and vicious. It is also what it completely believes itself to be. This priest "advises" a woman to her death. The poem calmly dramatizes, using the dialogue of the confessional, the true nature of spiritual tyranny.

Spiritual tyranny is a subtle thing. The first thing to say about it is that it usually works. The people who defend it most vigorously are its victims. That is why the "Irish Mother" of song and story, the bearer of infinite children, the heroine of countless ballads, is the first person to come to the defense of the Church's sexual policy which would use women mercilessly. Politically, sexual masochism is more effective than sexual sadism. Get a woman to "obey" till "death do you part", and you have her not only for wife but for life. In fact, at the moment, death is the only form of divorce in Ireland. When you have RIP after your name, you are a free man or woman.

The Church's exploitation of motherhood derives from its long use of the Mother of God, a most loving, patient, gentle, conscious and vigilant woman. So we have "Mother Ireland" just as we have "Mother Church" and even "Mother Machree". Mother. Mother. Mother.

Many Irish writers have tried to get to grips with the gentle tyranny of motherhood. In the following poem, I present a man who breaks free from the mothering-smothering forces in Irish society. When I read this poem on Irish Radio recently, there were many impassioned and indignant protests from Irish mothers. (Nevertheless, I have deep admiration for many of these women as individuals.) The poem is called *Moloney Up And At It.*

Right A couple with a donkey and cart at Lisdoonvarna Festival in County Clare. Every year, during the month of September, thousands of single people in search of a partner swarm to this pretty country town for what the tourist board calls the Festival of Bachelors, and the locals call the September crowd.

Below A mother comforts her child.

My soul from hell, the night the ould wan died,
Moloney said, I cried an' cried
Tears down. I'd been tied to her string
Through rack and hardship and the wild fling
O' youth, through manhood and the grey
Days when youth begins to slip away,
And now my addled heart and head
Were bound by the memory of the dead.

Well, anyway, after puttin' herself down
In the box, I went to the town
O' Lishtowel for a few drinks, and there
I met a Knockanore woman with red hair
And gamey eye. I made bold
And in a short time had told
Her my story. She cocked her ear and listened well.
We drank until the darkness fell
And for hours after. The talk
Spun on love. "Can I walk
A piece with you?" says I. "Moloney", says she,
"You're welcome to do what you like with me."
Fair enough! We left Lishtowel and struck the road,
Footin' it free over pothole
And gravel. The Knockanore woman was full o' guff
And harped on all the tricks o' love.
I upped with my question. She
Was willin' and free.
"Where would you like it?" says I. "Well", she said,
"God's green earth is a warm bed."
"Right you are, girl", says I.
It happened we were passin' by
Gale graveyard where my mother lay.
"What would you say
To this place?" says I. "Moloney", says she,
"If it's right with you, it's right with me."

Straightaway, I opened the gate and led
The Knockanore woman over the dead
O' seven parishes. Talk of a flyer!
Fasht as they come an' hot as fire!
She fell down on the soft clay
Of a fresh grave, and before I could say
A word, I was on the ground as well,
Goin' like the hammers o' hell!
'Twas only then I saw where I was.
On my mother's grave! But that was no cause
For panic, though I was a bit
Upset at first by the strangeness of it.
The Knockanore woman was happy as Larry,
And I was sparkin' and merry
As a cricket. "Yerra, you might
As well enjoy the gift o' the night
While you have the chance", I said
To myself, realisin' the dead are dead,
Past holiness and harms –
And the livin' woman was in my arms.

'Twas great fun
While it lasted, and it lasted long. The sun
Was startin' to climb the sky when we rose
Up and settled our clothes.
"How are you, girl?" says I.
"Yerra, fine", says she.
"'Twas a fine night", says I.
"'Twas so, but a bit cold towards mornin", says she,
"And I wouldn't mind a hot cup o' tay
This minute". "You're a wise woman", I said,

"Let them say whatever they say,
There's wan thing sure. 'Tis hard to bate the cup o' tay".
And then, "Wisht", I said,
Suddenly remembering the quiet dead.
With the memory, I started to sing,
Then and there, a bar of a jig,
And as I sang I danced as well
On the body whose soul was in heaven or hell.
"You're a gay man", says she, "to bring
Me to a place like this for your bit of a fling,
And I'm thinkin' the love has gone to your head
When you dance a jig on the bones o' the dead",
Said I, "By the Christ that is divine,
If I have a son may he dance on mine.
While a man has the chance he should dance and sing",
    I said,
"For he'll be the hell of a long time dead.
So come on now without further ado
And I'll put on the kettle for the tay".
She smiled and we started on our way
In the early light that was breakin' for day.
The night was lost, the daylight stretched ahead,
Behind me slept the unforgettable dead,
Beside me stepped a woman with gamey eye,
Laughin' as the sun mounted the sky.

Left This well-kept country churchyard is in Kilkenny.

Below Decorations such as these may be found on graves in churchyards around Ireland.

Thou shalt not. I often think about these words. Thou shalt not. There are times when I think that religion says only "Thou shalt not", and our ordinary human sexuality says simply "Thou shalt". And I think of these lines from my favourite poet, William Blake. The poem is called *The Garden of Love.*

I went to the Garden of Love,
And I saw what I never had seen:
A Chapel was built in the midst,
Where I used to play on the green.

And the gates of this Chapel were shut,
And "Thou Shalt Not" writ over the door:
So I turned to the Garden of Love,
That so many sweet flowers bore,

And I saw it was filled with graves,
And tombstones where flowers should be:
And Priests in black gowns were
walking their rounds,
And binding with briars, my joys and desires.

I would like to see Ireland flourish and grow into a true Garden of Love. That, after all, is the aim of Christianity. At the moment, Ireland is in danger of becoming a land of frustrated materialism powered by holy hypocrites. But there are healthy signs as well. Church and State are learning to respect the integrity of each other's separateness. Youngsters are talking again of all kinds of freedom. Ould fellas like me are learning from the young.

What I have been trying to express is that, in Ireland, sex has more to say to religion than religion has to say to sex. The message, once the complexities of the matter are grasped and meditated on, is simple and clear and enduring. Do not be afraid to love.

Brendan Kennelly

Left Demonstrators at an anti-amendment march in Dublin in March, 1983. Abortion has always been illegal in Ireland, but now it is also against the Constitution after an amendment was passed to write into the Constitution that abortion could not be made legal.

Below Exuberant young Catholics welcome Pope John Paul II when he arrived to take a youth Mass at Ballybrit racecourse near Galway City in 1979.

Calvary towers above the water on Slea Head, at the end of the Dingle peninsula. This is the most westerly point of Ireland; beyond are the gray waves of the Atlantic Ocean.

I t is important to keep in mind, when discussing the Irish character, that the island is very small: a mere 300 miles from its northernmost extremity to the far south, and little more than half that distance from east coast to west.

This "little room", in the words of W. B. Yeats, that led to "great hatred", contains a remarkable variety of landscape, with people who speak in a Babel of accents and some in two languages, the ancestral Irish as well as the more universal English.

Their ancestry is also reflected in their physical characteristics, their religious and social practices and in their customs. The diversity of their origins and the cultural forces to which they were subjected at various stages in history cause contradictions which, to some, are the yeast and salt in the national cake. Others, particularly those who like to reduce complex subjects to convenient generalizations, find these contradictions irritating and confusing.

Despite the work done by serious historians, film-makers and the more perceptive travel-writers, these convenient generalizations still abound to confuse rather than illuminate the path of the curious traveler. He who comes to observe the witty, golden-tongued Irish, in full flight of fancy in a typical village pub, would do well to choose carefully.

Once, in the Antrim village of Portglenone, I sat for a good half-hour one night and observed five men contemplating the froth on their glasses of stout and the loudly-ticking pub clock, during the course of which witticisms of this nature were exchanged:

"Brave an' coul' the night."

"Ach, aye."

"Brave an' coul' surely."

"Aye indeed, for the time o' year."

"Ach, aye, surely."

"No change, neither."

"Divil the change."

The drinkers were typical Irishmen of a certain regional culture and social class, as sparing of words as they were of the money in their pockets.

On the other hand, the traveler could just as easily happen upon a gaggle of men, hunched against the gable of a public house in the west of Ireland, filling the air with nervous eloquence and mirth, as they waited impatiently for pub opening-time.

These men would be typical of another

Left Aran Islanders display signs of their hybrid heritage.

Below Women generations ago would have looked much like this twentieth-century countrywoman.

social class and regional culture. To them, pleasant survival in a precarious world is far more important than any ethic concerning the work that may or may not be done on the morrow. It would also be true to say that a substantial majority of the population would fall between these two rather extreme stools and lie there somewhat anonymously, dully, contentedly . . .

The pint pot that is the island of Ireland has been forced to contain within it a veritable gallon of plunderers, colonizers, missionaries of different kinds, adventurers, refugees of various persecuted denominations and seekers after the wisdom that is believed to exist on the extremities of continents. All of them left some mark: very few of their shadows have faded without trace.

People take me for a typical Celt. "Ah! An Aran Islander!" they cry, "How very interesting. At last a *real* Irishman." But how real is "real", even in the case of one whose neighboring parish to the west is on the shores of America? I fear that when Robert Flaherty made *Man of Aran* he sent a cluster of myths into orbit and not all of them have burnt up on re-entry.

Without over-burdening the reader with details let us take a short-cut through the history of Aran. The Celts, having retreated to the extremities of Western Europe, are credited by some archaeologists with having built the large stone forts that dominate the island on which I grew up. Others give credit to the rather shadowy tribe that preceded them: archaeology, like anthropology and psychiatry, can sometimes be an intriguingly inexact discipline.

After the Christianization of Ireland and the Danish and Norman invasions, Aran became, in turn, a great monastic settlement, a small prize in a power-struggle between the warring Irish clans of O'Brien and O'Flaherty, an Elizabethan garrison, a Cromwellian prison, part of a landlord's fief and, from the end of the nineteenth century, a shrine for writers, linguists, archeologists, folklorists and would-be worshipers of the national and cultural tap-root.

Then, after three decades of independence, came the exact scientists. They sampled our blood, took impressions of our teeth, measured our heads and frames and went away to analyze their findings. To the consternation of those who had taken it upon themselves to categorize us as "true Celts", it was found that the typical islander closely resembled, in stature and in the structure of blood and bone, the native of East Anglia in England, and that his teeth closely resembled those of a typical Cockney from London.

The islanders, in fact, were displaying the signs of their hybrid heritage. The findings cheered them greatly for they removed that far more feared stigma of an inbred society.

Some anthropologists, who later came to

study our social habits, were inclined to regard our blessings as mixed. One of them wrote in an American journal, *Psychology Today*, in February 1971, that although he found no evidence "of childlessness based on the sexual ignorance of spouses" nevertheless, the people were blissfully ignorant of many uncommon sexual practices.

Which only goes to show that a fairly variegated people can survive for centuries on a remote rock in the Atlantic, without any of the more spectacular characteristics of the personae in a Harold Robbins novel. What it tells us about the science of anthropology scarcely calls for comment.

But not all of the national genes were scrambled so successfully. Some tribes arrived, conquered modest spoils and then sat fast on their gains until the present day, learning nothing and forgetting even less. Not by his Twelfth of July regalia alone (bowler hat, dark suit, sash and walking stick) shall the Northern Ireland Orangeman be known, but by the constancy and purity of his genes also. For the Northern Ireland situation is an example of diversity leading, not to richness, contradiction and change, but to polarization, suspicion and stagnation. When one takes away the bombs, the guns and the ferocious words that basic dilemma remains.

Not all national minorities were as introverted as the descendants of the seventeenth-century Northern planters. The Quakers and the Huguenots left their mark in Dublin and in the midland counties in a manner disproportionate to their numbers. The Jacobs,

Far Left This woman has her hands full looking after family, home and animals in the west of Ireland.

Below Many Irish people make their living from the sea that surrounds them.

Bewleys, Goodbodys and Odlums are among the most respected in the world of business and industry. Many of them, without sacrificing their principles or individuality, became deeply involved in social affairs as well.

A character in Joyce's *Ulysses* remarks that the Irish never persecuted the Jews, they just never let them come in. They certainly did not come in great numbers, but they did form active communities in Dublin, Belfast and Cork. To a greater extent than any of the other national minorities, Jewish involvement in Irish politics during and after the struggle for independence was unequivocal and sustained.

As well as providing two of the most popular and outspoken mayors of Dublin and Cork, three members of the present Dáil (parliament) come from Dublin's small Jewish community. And as if to prove their allegiance to different streams of political thought, they represent the three major political parties.

But to complete the picture, and to add yet another contradiction to the contemporary scene, the youngest member of the present Dáil is also the only Protestant in the assembly. Ivan Yates comes from the rural constituency of Wexford which contains a mere handful of Protestants. And, while too much can be made of individual examples in any

society, it would be fair as well as necessary to say that in public life in the Republic of Ireland it is what a person stands for, rather than his religion, ancestry or social standing, that matters when people are asked to vote for him.

That it is necessary to say so is in itself a comment on the face and mind of Ireland today. No other European state, not even the brand new German Democratic Republic, can match, for sheer selfconsciousness, the great debate on "Irishness" and the comparative importance of the various elements it contains. The contemporary violence in Northern Ireland has reactivated this debate and given it a reality it previously lacked.

It is an acrimonious debate, at times a dialogue of the deliberately deaf, but it does serve to concentrate the more open and reflective minds on what is divisive and what could be conducive to mutual understanding and peace in Irish life.

Unfortunately, like most such Irish debates, it is fast becoming an end in itself and, so far, the other party involved in Irish affairs (the British government) has taken no great heed of either the noise or what sense has emerged. It will eventually peter out in a falling cadence of exhausted clichés and the air will be left to echo with the sound of bombs and bullets and

Far Left Northern Irish Orangemen wear their distinctive sashes on July 12 each year when they celebrate "King Billy's" victory at the Battle of the Boyne.

Below A weaver spins the thread from which he will make cloth on a wheel that he has probably made himself.

Left Distinctive Irish red hair and freckles.

tribal slogans throughout the country.

But even if it does end in this way it will have provided further proof of the partial truth of Dr Johnson's remark, too often truncated in quotation; "The Irish are not in a conspiracy to cheat the world by false representations of the merits of their countrymen. No, Sir; the Irish are a fair people – they never speak well of one another."

Dr Johnson almost got it right. But he forgot, or failed to understand, that this extreme respect for truth in the most difficult of circumstances was often accompanied by an attitude, summarized by someone else as, "my country, right or wrong". This may be regarded as an extreme form of patriotism – and we know how much the learned Doctor detested that – or it can be classified as nationalism.

At the time of writing, it is almost obligatory to describe all manifestations of Irish nationalism as "pernicious", particularly when addressing a foreign audience. Be that as it may, it certainly brings to mind the image of the ancient Celt going naked into battle with complete knowledge of his inevitable but glorious defeat. His wars may indeed have been merry and his songs sad, and much of his glory

may have been achieved while battling unsuccessfully against insurmountable odds, but, for good or ill, his descendants in the island of Ireland still break out in an ancestral rash from time to time.

The ancestral language is Irish (sometimes called Gaelic, which is also the Irish form of football), a close cousin of Scots Gaelic and Manx, and a bit further removed from Welsh, Breton and Cornish. The Irish language began to die at the beginning of the seventeenth century, but what many generations thought to be its final death-rattle proved to be a clearing of the throat for yet another final rally.

Its modern revival was mainly due to the efforts of a small group of Protestant scholars who founded the Gaelic League almost a century ago. Chief among them was Dr Douglas Hyde, who later became first president of Ireland in 1938. He saw the language as a cultural unifying force in the island, but, despite his efforts, his organization became part of the struggle for national independence. This, in turn, led many Northern Unionists to regard the ancestral language as another manifestation of the firm whose aim was to deprive the Unionists of their political power and take them over. The fact that the island's first daily

Below An Irishman stops for a break while harvesting his crop of "murphies".

Left A country face at a horse fair.

newspaper in Irish is published in Belfast merely reinforces their suspicions.

In the Republic, the Irish language is described in the Constitution as "the first official language" and is an obligatory subject in schools, although no longer a failing subject in public examinations. The reality of this rather large assumption is that a man was recently sent to prison for contempt of court because he demanded a trial through the medium of Irish in the Donegal Gaeltacht. ("Gaeltacht" is the official term for the areas where Irish is the first language of the community and where the government conducts its affairs in Irish.)

Needless to say, the contradictions between the official attitude to the language and reality has given rise to much acrimony and occasional ribaldry. In the Republic an emerging middle class would like it to crawl away and die. They regard it as an anachronism and an impediment to their chief ambition; the accumulation of wealth and equal partnership in the English-speaking world. But as the country is already English-speaking anyway, their case has a hollow ring and the Irish language seems likely to survive for a while longer – certainly at least for another two or three generations.

Left The Irish language is in everyday use, and not only on telephone boxes.

Below This is the only surviving officer (and bugler) of Lord Hillsborough's Private Army, County Down, a garrison consisting of a sergeant and 20 men which was disbanded in 1890. His uniform may derive from the Dutch guards of William of Orange.

133

And whatever one may think of the efforts to revive it, the ancestral language is the most distinctively native (Celtic or Irish if you wish) manifestation of the continuity of life on the island. The fact that it is still a controversial matter, about which very patriotic citizens have mixed feelings, signifies a certain lust for life against the force of logic. It is also a very good reason for the traveler to avoid getting involved in arguments concerning its usefulness in the modern world.

Traditional Irish music should, on the face of it, be one of the great unifying forces in Ireland. To those who, rightly, regard it as one of the great folk music traditions of modern times, it may come as a surprise to learn that it almost died out in the third and fourth decades of this century. Neglect and a concerted effort to kill native entertainment in the homes of rural Ireland combined to drive the musicians, their music and the traditional set-dances virtually underground.

The Catholic clergy, who could spot an occasion of sin before the thought entered the

Right The fiddler with his traditional music attracts quite a crowd, even in the face of more modern competition.

mind of the potential sinner, decided that dancing should take place under their own eyes as far as was humanly possible. The traditional dances in houses, with music provided by local pipers, fiddlers and flute-players, were declared to be undesirable. For one thing they were not clerically supervised and, although the pastoral letters of the day cloak the unworthy thought in flowery language, it was clearly inferred that the perpendicular pleasures of the Irish Kitchen dance might lead to horizontal dalliance which could prove detrimental to body and soul, not to mention the good name of the country.

So it came to pass that almost every parish in rural Ireland, as well as most of the smaller towns, sprouted grey concrete ghastlinesses known as parochial halls. The faithful were encouraged to attend these places of entertainment where jazzbands provided the music, where proper behavior was enforced by a properly-trained cleric and where the takings swelled the parish funds.

It was very moral and it also was good

Above Young buskers play a duet in the sun. There is always music in the air in Ireland.

business. Indeed, so keen was the competition between two neighboring parochial halls that a strange story circulated through the length and breadth of Ireland (it has been calculated that it takes five days for a good rumor to travel, by word of mouth, from Malin Head in Donegal to Mizzen Head in Cork) during the early 1950s.

It concerned a young and innocent girl attending her first dance in one of the rival halls and the handsome young man who charmed her. She felt powerless in his arms and did not seem able to control her feelings as he tried to lure her to his car. Just as she was about to succumb she looked down, screamed loudly, crossed herself and fainted. The charming young man, whose cloven hoof had scared her out of more than a year's growth, vanished in a puff of sulfur through the roof of the dance hall. A year later, the grass was growing in its car-park and the birds were nesting in its rafters. The success of the state of business in

Left Young and old size up the horses at a fair in Listowel, Country Kerry.

the rival hall can be left to the imagination.

Radio Eireann (as the national broadcasting service was then called) decided to record what was left of the traditional music and broadcast the best of it. In so far as the revival of a vanishing tradition can be attributed to a single action, Radio Eireann can claim credit for the astonishing hold the music, song and dance took on the young people of Ireland in the late 1950s and early 1960s. The fact that the revival coincided with a period of affluence and greater social freedom, as well as a slowing down in the rate of emigration to Britain and the USA, provided an additional impetus.

An organization called Comhaltas Ceoltóirí Eireann (Federation of Irish Musicians) was founded to foster the revival, and one of its first acts was to organize great gatherings of musicians called a Fleadh Cheoil (literally a feast of music). These gatherings, at country and provincial level, drew great crowds and the annual

Right Two thatchers repair the roof
of a country cottage.

All-Ireland Fleadh began to attract attendances of almost 100,000. Most of these yearly pilgrims were teenagers.

Social commentators as well as one poet, at least, date the birth of the new attitude to culture, tradition and morals from the All-Ireland Fleadh Cheoil of 1963 which was held over the Whit weekend in the Midland town of Mullingar. The town was packed, there was music to be heard everywhere, indoors and out, but there was little or no disorder. On the Monday morning the local bishop condemned the event from the pulpit as a reprehensible and immoral gathering. After that, Comhaltas Ceoltóirí Eireann could only go from success to success; which it did, although the All-Ireland Fleadh suffered briefly from the modern worldwide phenomenon of mindless and destructive teenage thuggery.

It is impossible to write at any length about social life in Ireland without discussing drink. From birth to the final descent to the grave, drink is a constant factor at all Irish occasions.

Contemporary historians have noted the Celtic fondness for great quantities of wine and how their feasts often turned into bloody fights originating in boastful bragging concerning strength and valor.

Without wishing to be fanciful, let me bear witness to the fact that the Irish funeral is probably the most uniquely original and peaceful social occasion. Weddings frequently culminate in disorder, aided and abetted by the demon drink, but the funeral seems to bring out everything that is best in a complex nature. Not to give the departed a good, highly lubricated send-off is a grave social lapse on the part of family and friends, and one which will be remembered for years.

It is not surprising, therefore, that drink plays a large part in these congregations of musicians, aficionados and camp-followers. Mullingar was my first All-Ireland Fleadh and I had the benefit of a local guide's knowledge as well as the hospitality of his home: no small matter in a town where every available bed was

Below A cross-section of townspeople pause on a bench in a crowded Dublin street.

let out at the rate of a small apartment.

During the weekend he drew my attention to a small middle-aged man, dressed in a mildewed suit, once respectable, a hard hat and a Guinness-stained shirt which was once white.

He moved from pub to pub, always alone, always drinking stout out of the bottle. He never got tipsy, let alone drunk, and the only change in his appearance in the course of the weekend was the steady growth of ginger fleece on his mottled face.

"A hard case," said my friend; "his wife and children have left and there can be very little left now from the proceeds of the second farm. Two shops, two farms and a gravel pit. That's serious drinking for you. But a decent little man and it's nice to see him enjoying himself."

On Tuesday morning, as Mullingar emptied and as the newspapers carried full reports of the Bishop's denunciation, my friend and I met for a parting glass in a hotel in the center of the town. The traveling salesmen were moving west after the long weekend and, with the prurience which seems to be the hallmark of their calling in all countries, they sought details of the great feast of immorality they had missed by returning to the bosom of their families.

Right Passing time outside Sheehan's.

Below New times, new faces, in the city.

Right Happy young faces on a modern estate in Ballymun, Dublin.

142

Above Perfect solitude.

Already a rumor circulated in Dublin about a young man who, on the sweltering Sunday afternoon, having taken his pleasure with his willing lady on the banks of the canal, jumped in for a swim and was instantly stricken in his prime and mortal sinfulness. Did it really happen? Tell us! Tell us more!

Standing quietly beside me, the little man with the ginger fuzz signified that a helping hand with the price of a bottle of stout would be appreciated. Having thanked me civilly and having ministered to his obvious need, he spoke at length for the first time.

"What's all this talk about it being a bad Fleadh? I came into town at midday on Friday and I've walked the length of it umpteen times since – scarce closed an eye for more than an hour or two – and do you know what I'm going to tell you now? I seen no immorality at all. And I'll tell you something else. I think it was a great Fleadh. Only for the cursed music it would have been better than the Galway Races."

The faces of Ireland are not clearly seen. They are always slightly out of focus. This, as well as making them more interesting, is a reflection of what went before and what is happening now. For the only thing one can say with total certainty about the island of Ireland and its inhabitants is that it is – and will probably remain so for many years – unfinished business.

Breandán O hEithir

The President of Ireland, Dr Patrick Hillery, plays golf off a single-figure handicap and his aide-de-camp, Commandant Ciaran Fitzgerald, is the captain of the Irish rugby team. Jack Lynch, the former Prime Minister, won all the top honors available to him in Gaelic football and hurling. Ireland's best-known businessman, the president of Heinz, Tony O'Reilly, played rugby for Ireland and the British and Irish international teams, and the current vice-premier in the Government, Dick Spring, is another former international rugby player. The annual congress of the main opposition party in the Dáil, Fianna Fail, recently adjourned for three hours to allow the delegates to watch the Grand National steeplechase and the international rugby game between Ireland and England on television.

Sports are woven closely into the fabric of Irish life and, although there may be many who are not really interested in sporting endeavor, very few are prepared publicly to admit their ignorance. One of the criticisms leveled at the Prime Minister, Garret FitzGerald, is that he once admitted that he would prefer to study a train timetable than watch a football game. It is said that this unguarded statement cost him several points in a subsequent popularity poll.

Far Left Ireland tackle Wales during the 1985 rugby international.

Left Ciaran Fitzgerald, captain of the Irish rubgy team in 1985.

Sporting heroes are legion in folklore, in history and in song. A certain Thady Quill is immortalized in a ballad:

In the great hurling match between
* Cork and Tipperary,*
'Twas played in a field on the banks
* of the Lee.*
Our own darlin' hurlers afraid of
* being beaten,*
They sent for bould Thady to
* Ballinagree.*

Yerra he hurled the ball right and left
* in their faces*
And showed the Tipperary lads
* training and skill.*
If they trod near his lines shure he swore
* he would maim them*
And the papers were full of the praise
* of Thad Quill.*

For ramblin' for rovin' for football or
* courtin'*
For drinking black porter as fast as
* you fill.*
In all your day's rovin' you'll find
* none so jovial*
As the Muskerry sportsman the bould
* Thady Quill.*

The ballad has become something of an institution and, as with all Irish institutions, there is a somewhat mischievous tale to be told about it. Thady Quill has become a sporting folk hero because of the exploits outlined in the ballad but it appears that the inspiration for the song in real life was far from being a person of talent in any field, least of all sport. Laughter and mischief are never far away from the sporting scene and, even though sports are a deadly solemn pursuit at times, a smile is always lurking on the other side of the face. As Tony O'Reilly once said: "The condition of Irish sport is frequently desperate but never serious".

It caused some amusement in Ireland recently when the Australian government declared a national holiday when their team took the America's Cup from the Americans. National holidays, most of them unofficial, are declared much more frequently in Ireland; almost as frequently in fact as grandmothers' funerals. An obscure race meeting or a simple game of golf is often enough to cancel a board meeting or a day saving the harvest. Sports are a national obsession.

There is plenty of evidence in mythology and not a little in history to indicate that organized games took place in Ireland long before the ancient Olympic Games. A program of sporting events to honor Queen Tailte in the kingdom of Meath called the Tailteann Games was organized several centuries before the Greek Olympics. Running, jumping, throwing the spear or javelin and hurling were all on the bill

Right Brian O'Donnell, from County Galway, playing Gaelic football in 1984.

in the Tailteann Games. It is recorded in the old Irish legends that admission to the Fianna, Fionn MacCumhail's traveling militia, was allowed only to those who excelled in such sporting pursuits. The historian Brother Liam P. O. Caithnia has, in his research, come across references to hurling and other games in the ancient Brehon Laws, in the sagas of the Red Branch Knights and the *Fenian* or *Ossianic Cycle* of legends.

It is a somewhat refined version of hurling which survives and thrives in Ireland today and which attracts as many as 70,000 people to the top contests. A distinctively Irish game, it is contested with great fervor and elan; sometimes wild, sometimes as smooth and elusive as gossamer, prompting many commentators to refer to it as an art form. Played with a leather-covered ball about the same size as a tennis ball and with curved sticks fashioned with great skill and care from the roots of ash trees, its speed is bewildering to the uninitiated as the ball flies from one end of the field to the other, driven through the air or on the ground with dexterity and blinding speed.

It was at this game that the former Prime Minister Jack Lynch excelled, winning five All Ireland medals with Cork in the 1940s. But even he pales as a hero before the challenge of his team-mate Christy Ring around whom legends have grown up and about whom books have been written and to whom a life-sized statue has been erected. Not even a Prime Minister can be as famous as Christy Ring. His reputation for turning looming defeat into last-minute victory is also the stuff of balladry:

Now Cork are beat,
The day is saved,
The Tippmen stoutly sing.
You spoke to soon,
My sweet gossoon,
For here comes Christy Ring!

Another great hero of earlier times was Tommy Daly, a doctor from Clare. He was a goalkeeper and, if you have to be a bit mad to be a good hurler, you have to be completely insane to play in goal. In Daly's days goalkeepers were not protected by the rules. Once the match started, "open season" was declared on the goalkeepers and the only protection they had was a wall of bodies provided by their defending colleagues. Even now a goalkeeper has to have the eyes of a hawk, hands like a magnet, nerves of steel and bones of tungsten. The ball comes whizzing in at speeds of up to 70 or 80 miles an hour. It has to be stopped with stick or hand to prevent a goal and then driven away as opponents bear down, intent on creating mayhem.

Goalkeepers don't mind that so much. Footwork and speed of thought can get a man out of trouble. What they really fear is the high ball dropping sharply into the goalmouth. Then the nerves and the eye are tested to the full; the ball

Left Hurling is an immensely popular – and extremely aggressive – national sport.

Above Alex "Hurricane" Higgins, moody genius on the snooker table, and winner of numerous competitions.

Right Unlike soccer, but like rugby and American football, Gaelic football involves hands just as much as feet. It is even more popular as a national sport than hurling, despite being a staid cousin of hurling. Spectators flock to see games, especially at the conclusion of the annual All-Ireland championship in August and September.

must be the only focus of attention. Not until it is grabbed out of the forest of ashen sticks can personal safety or concern for life and limb be taken into account.

When Tommy Daly was playing for his native Clare, and later for Dublin, the goalkeeper could be challenged with shoulder and thigh either when he was in possession of the ball or without it, and he could be driven physically into the goalnet for a goal. The area around the goal came to be known as Hell's Kitchen. In high summer with the grass worn from the goal area, clouds of dust would rise as fierce contests took place.

On one such occasion a Tipperary goalkeeper called Tony Reddan was bundled without ceremony into the goal for a score by Jack Lynch. Lynch had, just a few weeks earlier, been elected to the Dáil for the first time. Reddan rose from the net as Lynch retreated to his position. Reddan fixed him with a beady eye and, shaking his hurley stick fiercely in Lynch's direction, he yelled: "Come in here again like that, Lynch, and there'll be an early by-election!"

Gaelic football, often referred to as a mixture of soccer, rugby and American gridiron, is a somewhat staid cousin of hurling and is even more widespread and popular. Instead of being described as a mixture of the other games it would probably be more correct to say that it is the begetter of them all, for there are many reasons to suggest that it predates them. The big games at the conclusion of the All-Ireland championship take on the trappings of national occasions in August and September.

Left George Best from Belfast, playing for the Aztecs against the Cosmos in America.

Far Right John Treacy running for Ireland.

Below Mary Peters, from Belfast, is Ireland's most famous woman athlete. She won a gold medal in the women's pentathlon during the 1972 Olympics in Munich.

For the purposes of this competition the teams represent the counties in which the players are born and keen rivalry has built up over the years. The classic county/city confrontation between Kerry and Dublin in football in recent times has electrified the country in high summer. Part of the spin-off has been a spate of "Kerry jokes" in which the smart city slicker pokes fun at the innocent rural Kerryman. Kerry jokes in Ireland are Paddy jokes in England or Polak jokes in the US. But a Kerryman recently turned the laugh against the Dubliners. "Have you heard the latest Kerry joke?" he said, and then supplied the answer: "The Dublin football team, of course!"

The traditional games have given the Irish sports scene a unique flavor and a sturdy base on which to display the national character. But internationally, too, the Irish can be observed at play notably on the athletics track where, for a small country, a high standard has been set. In recent times, Eamon Coghlan has dominated the indoor scene in the United States and added the world 5000 meters championship to his list of victories at Helsinki in 1983. John Treacy won a silver medal in the marathon event at the Los Angeles Olympics. It was in Los Angeles that Ireland's finest Olympic hour was recorded as far back as 1932, when two Tipperary athletes won Olympic golds within an hour of each other – Pat O'Callaghan in the hammer event and Bob Tisdall in the 400 meter hurdles.

Throwing the hammer is said to be another Irish sport which was dominated by Irish athletes up until 1932. Many of these Irishmen

were competing for the United States. Oddly enough, that 1932 victory was Ireland's last win in the event and the saddest factor of Irish life was partly responsible, that factor being divisive politics. An observer will get a laugh out of almost any facet of Irish life but mention of the border in so far as it impinges on sports will not bring even the ghost of a smile.

The border has had a deadening effect on many Irish sports organizations, notably soccer and athletics. Frequent efforts are made to heal "The Split" in these and other sporting bodies without much success. The games of hurling and Gaelic football already mentioned are not divided, mainly because they are part of the nationalist-Catholic tradition. Strangely enough, rugby, too, has not been divided in spite of all sorts of political upheaval.

Rugby started out in Ireland as an exclusive Protestant and "garrison" game but the adoption of the game by Catholic upper-class schools changed the emphasis greatly and it is now a game for people of all backgrounds, politics and religions.

It is on a rugby international day in Dublin that Ireland shows a face to the world which indicates what a united Ireland might be like.

Both on and off the field Catholic, Protestant, dissenter, Unionist and Republican, Socialist and Conservative, Liberal and bigot mix into an attractive amalgam of faces, attitudes and accents. On the field Irish Army men and Royal Ulster Constabulary members play in the green, shamrock-sprigged shirts and stand shoulder to shoulder facing the Tricolour for an anthem which includes the lines:

Below Supporters from Cork enjoy the sunshine during a hurling game.

Tonight we'll man the bearna baoil*
Let Erin's call come woe or weal.
Mid cannon's roar and rifle's peal
We will chant A Soldier's Song.
*Gap of danger.

Rugby has not been without its political problems. In 1953 at an international game in Belfast, Irish supporters carrying the Irish Tricolour were attacked by RUC officers attempting to enforce a legal ban on that flag in Northern Ireland. A riot was only narrowly averted. Irish rugby seemed to be on the brink of the abyss over which so many other sporting links had gone. Cool heads won the day, however, but all international games are now played in Dublin and the Lansdowne Road stadium has become a symbol for Irish

sporting friendship across the border.

Sadly, attempts to repeat this in other sports have failed. Two international soccer teams are fielded in competitions like the World Cup. At club level in Northern Ireland sectarianism is rife at football games. Two teams from Nationalist areas have been forced out of soccer entirely. Songs of a sectarian nature are used to taunt opposition supporters: "We'll kick 10,000 Papishes all over Dolly's Brae" is one of the less offensive ditties.

It is perhaps in the presence of horses and greyhounds that the Irishman reveals his sentimentality. Love for these animals is perhaps too mean a word: devotion might fit better. The bones of Arkle, one of the great steeplechasers, have been dug up and reassembled in skeleton form at the National Stud in Kildare. A statue to that great coursing greyhound Master McGrath stands by the roadside in Waterford.

The top race-meetings at places like the Curragh, Leopardstown, Phoenix Park, Fairyhouse and Tralee and dozens of other tracks dotted around the country are thronged even on working days. Thousands of people flock to

Right The Irish are devoted supporters of horse racing, and flock to the race courses in their thousands to bet huge sums of money.

Above Arkle, the famous steeplechaser whose bones were exhumed to stand in state at the National Stud in Kildare.

Galway for a five-day meeting in July every year. Millions of pounds are bet on the horses; all-night poker games with drinking and musicianship thrown in go on all night.

Again the mix of class and creed is fully representative of all sections of a diverse community. Priests and paupers will mingle with millionaires and charlatans; the presence of pickpockets is regarded as an inevitable, if undesirable, evil.

A day at the races is not just racing; it is living. Fortunes may be lost but there is always tomorrow when luck will surely change. The next generation of horse-lovers will be there

with their lollipops watching the Punch and Judy Show.

Information is an important word in racing circles. A man who has this elusive commodity has a meal and drink ticket. He will not come out directly with this information, but will convey his views on the winner of the next race through nods and winks and ambiguous innuendo. This is to guard against a charge later of giving "wrong information". If direct news is not conveyed then the dispenser can always claim to have been misinterpreted.

Above all, race meetings for either dogs or horses are mainly "for the crack". Crack is another word which conveys a great variety of meaning. Crack is fun, "divilment", song, dance, drink, music, laughter, lies and rumors. One Irishman who enjoyed "the crack" greatly until it all got too much for him was Jack Doyle, a swashbuckling Corkman who made a fortune with his fists, lost it again, turned himself into a cabaret act in sleazy nightclubs and died penniless.

Doyle was a bit of a braggart but a likeable one, a rogue with a big heart in a big body. He boasted once during the height of his career as a boxer-cum-entertainer that: "I can sing like John McCormack and box like Jack Dempsey". When the news was given to Dempsey

his scathing reply was: "I think the guy has got it the wrong way around".

Doyle was larger than life. He married the tempestuous movie star Movita and the streets of Dublin and Cork were jammed when he brought her home to show the neighbors. But high living, late nights and boxing don't mix. Doyle's horizontal approach to life both inside and outside the ring, drunk or sober, soon took their toll. Hundreds of men of his generation will tell you still of the half crown they lent Jack Doyle when he was down and out and parched for the want of a drink.

Not all Irish boxers ended up like Doyle. The descendants of Irish parents like John L. Sullivan and Gene Tunney made fortunes at the sport and are listed in the pantheon of great heavyweights. In a small pub in the town of Kilcullen in the county of Kildare the mummified arm of an old-style bare-knuckle boxer called Dan Donnelly is preserved in a glass case. It is stared at reverently by thousands of

tourists while his exploits are recounted for their benefit.

Not far away a secluded small valley staged one of the most famous events in the history of Irish sport. It was there in 1815 that Donnelly took on the pride of England, George Cooper, and beat him into subjection in 11 bloody rounds. More than 30,000 spectators were crammed into the valley which has been known ever since as "Donnelly's Hollow". He, like Doyle, loved the bright lights and the fame which his exploits brought him. He was vulnerable to flattery and to the depredations of borrowers and boyos, and he succumbed to all this and ill health as well before he could

Left Jack Doyle, photographed here in 1936, was a very popular, though unsuccessful, heavyweight boxer. He became famous for his rendering of Irish songs in the ring, and boasted that he could "sing like John McCormack and box like Jack Dempsey". Dempsey thought different.

Far Left World featherweight champion Barry McGuigan celebrates with his wife Sandra and son Blair after a strenuous fight in the ring in 1985.

Above Christy O'Connor putts during a match in 1967.

Right Joe Carr, a former Walker Cup player, drives off the tee at St Andrews in 1971.

truly test his mettle against the top boxers of the day.

There are very few Irish people who have not at one time tried sport of one kind or another. Golf, like rugby, has become a game for the masses. Thousands of golfers flock to clubs at weekends and at first light take on the scores of top-class courses all over the country. Everyone wants to be as good as Christy O'Connor or Joe Carr and if they can't quite play as well as those two they will be sure to "talk a good game". There is an urge in every Irishman to be a top sportsman: academic, financial or political success will always be regarded as secondary. A man who hasn't played hasn't quite made it in life.

This approach is epitomized in a tale about one Tom "Click" Brennan who as a young man played fervent football for his native county of Sligo, frequently referred to as "The Yeats County". Some years ago when "Click" was no longer young he met a young hitchhiker with a

pack on his back who wanted to know the road to Sligo town.

"Why do you want to go there?" Click asked.

"I'm going to the Yeats Summer School" the lad replied. "You know about Yeats? Sligo's most famous son. The Nobel Prizewinner."

"Yeats? Yeats?" said Click scratching his head, pretending not to know. "Famous Sligoman, was he? Well, I'll tell you this. Whoever he was he never kicked a ball for Sligo."

Failure comes in many guises. Failure at sport in Ireland is the heaviest cross to bear.

Sean Kilfeather

Above The golf course at Ballybunion, on the coast of County Kerry, is one of Ireland's many beautiful courses.

Left A more beautiful spot could not have been chosen for a day's fishing. This man is tidal fishing for salmon and sea trout in Renvyle, County Galway.

Above Absolute quiet is vital when out shooting duck, as here, in County Wicklow.

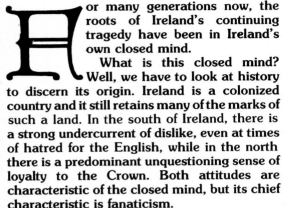

The Way Forward

For many generations now, the roots of Ireland's continuing tragedy have been in Ireland's own closed mind.

What is this closed mind? Well, we have to look at history to discern its origin. Ireland is a colonized country and it still retains many of the marks of such a land. In the south of Ireland, there is a strong undercurrent of dislike, even at times of hatred for the English, while in the north there is a predominant unquestioning sense of loyalty to the Crown. Both attitudes are characteristic of the closed mind, but its chief characteristic is fanaticism.

A fanatic is a terrorist who is himself terrified of alternatives. A fanatic is a person who can see only one point of view and who sincerely believes that other points of view are not merely wrong but have to be exterminated; they are evil since they threaten his own beliefs. The only way which the fanatic understands of coping with reality is the annihilation of those who disagree with him: to be different is to be worthy of destruction. A fanatic always wishes to bend reality to his own peculiar design. He will work with unrelenting energy and dedication to achieve this. He has complete strength and sincerity on his side. He is, in fact, incapable of insincerity. And he also has an even more powerful weapon to aid him in his "noble task", his "armed struggle", his "ancient enterprise". The fanatic has a mind that is completely closed.

In the Republic, the chief advocate of the closed mind is the Catholic Church. The Protestant Church, that is the Church of Ireland, is equally closed in its own way; but it has little or no power. The Church of Ireland is at once sophisticated and irrelevant, though it has produced a few brave spokesmen such as W. B. Stanford, Archbishop Simms, Douglas Gageby, Dean Victor Griffin, Shane Ross and Bishop Poyntz. Southern Irish Protestants, on the whole, are a mealy-mouthed lot, smilingly non-committed. They often seem scared and silent. Why don't they speak out? Why do they avoid this vital act of responsibility? Because of the closed mind.

The closed mind, though extremely firm, contained and resolute in itself, in its own defined context, is in fact terrified of expression, especially of expression coming from "strangers", "odd-balls" and "foreigners". Most of the Irish "odd-balls" have been Irish writers who tried to understand and express

Left Colored lights from street lamps are reflected on the wet pavements of O'Connell Street, Dublin, early one morning in February.

Right The Falls at Ennistymon in County Clare.

their country. In the 1930s, 1940s and 1950s, nearly every Irish writer worth his or her salt was banned by the Censorship Board. Thanks be to God, the same Censorship Board seems to have censored itself into a state of non-existence, or at least of acceptable paralysis, at the moment. These men and women, intelligent and terrified, were the intellectual representatives of the closed mind. They produced almost nothing and banned a lot of good literature. They were apostles of mediocrity. An American friend of mine, an academic, once said to me, "If I wanted a good reading-list of twentieth-century Irish writers, I think I'd simply give my students a list of all the books that have been banned in Ireland".

The closed mind never likes to rock the boat of its own security. In any sphere, it hates and fears the thought or image of a possible rival. It wants power and dominance. It craves the conviction that it alone is the sole embodiment of the truth. And, of course, if you exclude others, you may well become, in your own eyes at least, that very embodiment. To close up is to become isolated, convinced and strong. In Ireland, people have often and methodically closed their minds, fostered by the Catholic Church. Celibacy is the sexual equivalent of the closed mind.

If you wish to grow, if you wish to develop and change, you must enter into the thoughts and beliefs of those who are profoundly, and sometimes hurtfully, different from you. Difference is healthy, but the Irish Catholic Church hates and loathes difference. That means it will not develop and grow, and it will not allow its people to develop and grow, either. This is wrong, and should be put right.

The mark of any soul is its capacity for growth. God never created anything that had not the potential for growth. It is sinful and criminal to restrict that potential, but that restriction is the function of the closed mind. In the north of Ireland, people are murdering each other with increasing skill and dedication, because they have closed minds. Catholic and Nationalist; Protestant and Unionist. Labels: Ireland is an island of labels. In that situation, a man is not a man, but a label, and he will kill on behalf of his particular label.

It is necessary to grasp the intensity and strength of the closed mind. It does not question itself, but puts itself beyond the painful reaches of self-doubt. It assumes that its own self is the center of rightness, of infallibility. It knows right and wrong, it judges, it concludes. And so it can kill with impunity and defend with integrity.

Below A terrace of houses presents a closed front to the world at Clifden in County Galway.

Above The stadium is packed with people from all walks of life at the start of a match.

When Shakespeare wrote *Macbeth,* he believed a murderer must have pangs of conscience. But then Shakespeare never came to Ireland, or perhaps never met the closed mind. If he did, he turned his back on it, and he was right. In Ireland you cannot turn your back on the closed mind, because it is everywhere. On radio, on television, in newspapers, in pubs, in churches, in schools, in universities, in homes, in oneself. Even in sport.

Sport is one of the few areas where various forms of prejudice tend not to show themselves. When men and women confront each other in sport, they leave behind many of the prejudices that degrade and narrow their ordinary lives. Because sport is a matter of fiery passion and skill, prejudice gets burned up in it like old newspapers at a children's bonfire. Sport purifies and ennobles; but in Ireland, sad to say, it has also shown the

Above Rosettes and flags on sale during the All-Ireland final in 1984.

closed mind at work.

I will not dwell on this because I believe that the entire scene is slowly changing. And yet the Gaelic Athletic Association (the GAA), the most powerful sporting body in Ireland, is still not opening itself as it should to the *entire* youth of Ireland. The old entrenchment in self still exists.

In the 1940s and 1950s, you could not attend rugby or soccer games, if you were a member of the GAA. That seems incredible now. But that is what I'm talking about. The old hatred of difference, of alternatives. Cut out everybody else, show your own strength, emphasize your own ignorance, show your contempt, close your mind.

James Joyce's short story, *The Dead*, concerns people with closed minds. Some critics have said this is the greatest short story in the English language, and there is an argument to be put forward for that. One thing, however, which cannot be denied, is that it succeeds brilliantly as a scrutiny of people who have shut their minds to everything except their own petty realities. The "hero" of the story, Gabriel Conroy, discovers this truth near the end when he catches a glimpse of himself in the mirror of the hotel bedroom where he has gone, after a party, with the intention of making love to his wife, Gretta. But she, remembering a lover of many years ago, ignores him. Gabriel gets a glimpse of his closed, restricted life.

Since Joyce, many Irish writers have been savage in their attacks on this narrowness, this castrating, claustrophobic puritanism. People such as John McGahern, Edna O'Brien, Hugh Leonard, John Broderick, John B. Keane, Kevin Casey, Brendan Behan and a host of younger novelists, playwrights and short-story writers have lashed out at the constricting and debilitating effects of the closed minds and hearts of Ireland.

I think it can be said with justice and accuracy that Irish writers have nearly always

Above Author and playwright Brendan Behan (1923-1964) was born in Dublin. His most famous works include *Borstal Boy, The Quare Fellow* and *The Hostage*.

Right An aerial view of the Halfpenny Bridge over the River Liffey in central Dublin.

stood up for full freedom of expression. Sean O'Faolain and Peadar O'Donnell, who edited *The Bell*, a fiery, intelligent, open-minded journal, are good examples of this. So are Frank O'Connor, the towering Yeats and Joyce, and poets such as Patrick Kavanagh and Austin Clarke. Austin Clarke, especially, had the searing eye of the satirist for the terrified respectability characteristic of the closed mind. The following poem concerns the burial of an Irish President, Dr Douglas Hyde, a Protestant, a fine scholar, folklorist and translator of Irish poetry. In this poem, his body lies in St Patrick's Cathedral, a beautiful Protestant Cathedral in Dublin, where the great Dean Swift once ministered. Outside the Cathedral are members of the Irish Government, hiding, because Catholics committed grave sin if they ventured into Protestant centers of worship. This poem, *Burial Of An Irish President*, is one of the most savage indictments of that closed mind which has so effectively impeded the progress and development of Ireland.

Above This portrait of the author James Joyce (1882-1941) was painted by Jacques Emile Blanche. (National Portrait Gallery, London.)

> The tolling from St Patrick's
> Cathedral was brangled, repeating
> Itself in top-back room
> And alley of the Coombe,
> Crowding the dirty streets,
> Upbraiding all our pat tricks.
> Tricoloured and beflowered,
> Coffin of our President,
> Where fifty mourners bowed,
> Was trestled in the gloom
> Of arch and monument,
> Beyond the desperate tomb
> Of Swift. Imperial flags,
> Corunna, Quatre Bras,
> Inkermann, Pretoria,
> Their pride turning to rags,
> Drooped, smoke-thin as the booming
> Of cannon. The simple word
> From heaven was vaulted, stirred
> By candles. At the last bench
> Two Catholics, the French
> Ambassador and I, knelt down.
> The vergers waited. Outside,
> The hush of Dublin town,
> Professors of cap and gown,
> Costello, his Cabinet,
> In Government cars, hiding
> Around the corner, ready
> Tall hat in hand, dreading
> Our Father *in English. Better*
> *Not hear that "which" for "who"*
> *And risk eternal doom.*

As I understand the matter, the way forward for Ireland is to fight this closed mind and all its secure, vicious implications. What does one do with a closed mind? Open it up. And there are increasingly healthy signs that the mind of Ireland is opening.

First of all, it is impossible to understand Ireland without thinking of England. They are physically close and politically bound up, but they have never really spoken to one another. However, they are beginning to speak to each other, to communicate.

England is a great country, but in its dealings with Ireland it has often been deaf, boorish and ignorant. We Irish, in our turn, have often been vicious and violent in our dealings with England and the English.

We must learn to speak to each other, to talk things out. It is the only way.

173

There is a lot of abstract hatred in Ireland, which needs to be got rid of. We must learn instead to relate and to understand. We are a nation of talkers, but are we a nation of communicators? I would say that we talk a lot but communicate relatively little. Above all, in the interest of our political development, we need to communicate with the English, and the English must learn to communicate with us. Otherwise, there is only violence and folly and the huge boom of the bomb that speaks of nothing but maiming and death.

In their dealings with the Irish, the English have frequently been churlish and insensitive. "Out, out, out!" is now a famous phrase of Mrs Thatcher's. There is a boorish impatience and dismissal in those words, but "Bomb, bomb, bomb!" is not the answer to that crude dismissal: the answer lies in creative and sympathetic

Left Stormont, by Sir Arnold Thornley, was built outside Belfast in 1932 to house the Northern Ireland parliament, which was suspended in 1972.

dialogue. It is going to be very difficult because *all* sections must be allowed to speak.

It is pointless not to allow groups like the IRA and the UVF to have their say, to assert simply that such people are terrorists and should not be listened to by "ordinary, decent people". Many "ordinary, decent people" practice their own forms of terrorism.

The IRA should be invited to speak to the Irish people, and the Irish people allowed to speak back. Television is an excellent medium for this. What we need is full, honest communication, not murderous bombs. Do not isolate subversives and terrorists and revolutionaries. Let them speak to the people they are claiming to liberate, and let the people speak back. Then we may begin to discover who is liberating whom. We will begin to find out what is really wanted. And instead of killing each other, perhaps we can work towards a new, tolerant Ireland where every voice is

Above Communication is being established: British Prime Minister Mrs Thatcher shakes hands with Irish Taioseach Garret FitzGerald during talks.

Above Ireland is a land of immense beauty. Here a man tends his cattle by the side of a lough.

Right A tanker nears completion in the Harland & Wolff shipyard in Belfast. The ill-fated Titanic was also built in this shipyard.

heard and respected. I am not speaking about some vague Utopia: I am talking about a small island in the Atlantic that has not yet learned how to be truly tolerant; a tiny country that is full of promise.

England is a tolerant land. Thousands upon thousands of Irishmen appreciate that fact. England saved many an Irish family from hunger and despair in the 1930s, 1940s and 1950s, but as far as Ireland is concerned, England is not a good listener.

It doesn't *listen* to us as it should, that is, in a spirit of goodwill and understanding. Or when it does listen, that act of compassionate listen-

ing is too brief. To the English, the "Irish problem" is only one of many problems. To many Irish people, the "Irish problem" is of paramount importance.

In all this, a most important consideration is the matter of the Ulster Unionist. Here, too the need for dialogue, rather than merely talking *at* each other, or not talking at all, is of prime importance. The Ulster Unionists are a strong, proud, dominant people. But they must think out their position. And they must articulate it fairly and squarely. And the IRA must talk back, fairly and squarely. And the Government of the Republic must speak out in the

same manner, fairly and squarely.

The continuing tragic situation in Ireland is a classic example of people refusing to speak openly to each other. Many young people, bored and appalled at the futile bombing and killing, wish to enter into an intelligent dialogue with each other. I can foresee a Youth Movement coming into existence soon. It will speak of peace, not war; tolerance, not oppression; love not hatred.

Ireland is a country for young men and young women. They are beginning to sense their own power for good. Their minds are opening. Yet their situation is difficult. Many of them are unemployed. Unemployment is an insult to human dignity. Most people want to work. Most people deeply *need* to work. Unemployment is a chronic waste of energy and talent. It is also a source of cynicism, depression and despair.

There is a lot of unemployment in Ireland now. There is more crime than ever before. A lot of crime is committed out of boredom. Boredom is generated by unemployment. Unemployment leads to crime. I believe it is criminal of a government to allow unemployment to rise at the rate it is rising in Ireland at present.

Yet, in spite of that, many young Irish people are thinking and talking in a fluent, creative way about their country. They see that patriotism need not, should not involve assassination and mindless murders. They see that work and the dignity that goes with working are vital to a true, practical and visionary patriotism. The best patriot is the best worker. And many young people in Ireland are simply ravenous

Right Ireland's youth is its future.

Above Modern city buildings.

for work. Attention must be paid to this fact. If attention is paid, crime will diminish. Peace will be possible.

Most important of all, however, in the battle against the closed mind, is the need for education. Traditionally, the Irish are great lovers of education. They have gone in search of it all over Europe. Today, however, education is largely in the hands of the middle classes whereas it should be available to everyone. Education is still a matter of money whereas it should be a matter of talent, of intelligence and of desire.

We must open all our universities to all our people. Money should not be necessary to get into a university. There is only one necessary

qualification. Ability. If a boy or a girl has the ability, he or she should be given the opportunity. This is only just. But Irish politicians lack the imagination to see this simple fact. Or if they see it, they lack the heart to implement it. And yet, already, in spite of crippled, ambitious politicians, there are great advances in education, particularly among older people.

Education is about the discovery and the development of one's nature, character and personality. It concerns the bringing-out into the light of day all these talents which are buried in us. Some people do not sense these buried talents until they are well advanced in years.

A good educational system will enable people to discover and develop these hidden talents. And people should be able to do this at any point in their lives.

Education should not be confined to the young. It should be available to people at their moment of need, at whatever moment in their lives they feel they need it. This may happen at 16 or at 60.

I teach in a university. Some of the best students I have seen were people older than myself. In their studies, they taught me. Education is about eternal learning. We teach each other all the time. That is true teaching, true learning.

Adult education is strong in Ireland now. People who have raised families are going back to school. And in doing so they are not only stimulating themselves; they are enlightening youngsters who are younger than their own children.

This notion that education is not confined to the young, that it does not exist simply so that one can get a job, is vital. Neither is education a luxury or a rich privilege. Education is normal, difficult, enjoyable, civilized. People have a right to it.

There is a drift towards this kind of thinking in contemporary Ireland.

One day, any intelligent Irish boy or girl, man or woman, will be able to walk into any one of our universities and say "I wish to study Irish or English or French or Medicine or Engineering".

That day is not too far away. But we must work to bring that day closer. It is a day of justice. In modern Ireland, some of the people who have worked hardest for justice are women. If I single out Nell McCafferty, it is only because she has shown more aggressive energy than most others. Nell is a born writer and her campaign on behalf of women is really a campaign on behalf of justice. She is a model for Irish girls. She has her own voice, she is her own woman. She is hard-working, independent, fiery, true to her own vision. She'll put all the old stifling Irish Mothers (Mother Ireland, Mother Church, Mother Machree) where they belong. Nowhere. Nell is in the tradition of

Left Irish schoolgirls laugh happily as they walk home on a sunny afternoon.

Below Queen's University, by Charles Lanyon, is a Victorian red brick mock-Tudor building in Belfast. The central tower is very similar to the Founder's Tower at Magdalen College, Oxford, England.

Countess Markievicz, Lady Gregory, Maud Gonne MacBride, Bernadette Devlin and Sister Stanislaus Kennedy.

Miraculously, Ireland has always produced such women. They are strong when others are weak. They are valorous when others are cowardly and subservient. Nell McCafferty's writings about law and justice are among the most important documents out of Ireland over the past 50 years. Women are becoming concerned with law and justice. Why wouldn't they? For too long they were victims. Now they are thinkers.

Irishwomen are beginning to make their mark in literature too. Kate O'Brien, Mary Lavin and Edna O'Brien led the way. They are being followed by such women as Eavan Boland, Eilean Ni Chuilleanain, Maeve Kelly, Ann Hartigan, Paula Meehan, Julia O Faolain, and others.

Left A traditional Irish country figure walking home, heavily laden, accompanied by her two dogs.

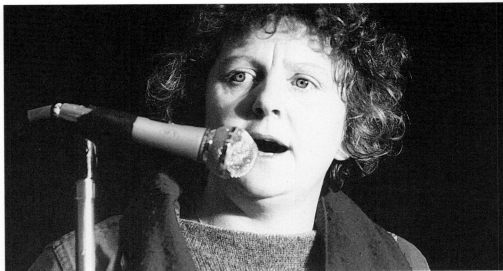

The subservient Irish woman is slowly becoming a creature of the dim and distant past. The new Irishwoman is a thinker. She may even help us Irishmen to grow up.

Growing up is difficult. Ireland is growing up. Sometimes I think it is growing up against its will. Sometimes I think it prefers to destroy itself. Why can't the IRA and the UVF and the INLA see that they are not *helping* Ireland to grow up? Why can't they see they are not *helping* themselves or anyone else?

If patriotism means anything, surely it is a kind of communal charity, a sort of casual helping-each-other, something normal and consistent and good-willed.

We must learn to help each other in this way. Catholic and Protestant and Jew, Unionist and Nationalist, city people and country people, Church and State – all must work together to produce the new Ireland, the Ireland that will emerge from trouble and darkness, from tragedy and suspicion and oppression and intolerance. We have to make a journey away from this and into tolerance.

Above Nell McCafferty is a witty, warm and outspoken feminist from Derry. She used to be a journalist for the Irish Times.

Tolerance is a beautiful country but the journey towards it is arduous and self-challenging. That is the difficult journey Ireland has to make.

Instead of killing, we must create. Instead of hating, we must love. This may seem a romantic dream. It is not. It is a real possibility. But to achieve it, we must get rid of the closed mind for good and for glory. We must open up to each other, especially to what we sense is most difficult and different in each other. If we do this we will discover the Ireland in our hearts: not a sentimental land, not a place to sing sloppy ballads about, not a gossipy, cynical little island, but a keen, intelligent, beautiful country with people who, knowing each other's creeds, beliefs and politics, are prepared, in the thoughtful goodness of their hearts and minds, to tolerate each other.

That is not Utopia.

That is Ireland.

Brendan Kennelly

Left The village of Clifden, County Galway, nestles in a hollow between the hills.

A happy family walk up the streets on Tory Island, off the north coast of Ireland.

INDEX

BIBLIOGRAPHY

Bradley, Anthony, *William Butler Yeats*, 1979, The Frederick Unger Publishing Co.

Brown, Terence, *Ireland: A Social and Cultural History*, 1981, Fontana.

Clarke, Austin, *Flight to Africa*, 1963, Dolmen Press.

de Breffny, Brian (Ed.), *Ireland: A Cultural Encyclopedia,* 1983, Thames & Hudson.

Facts about Ireland, 1985, Department of Foreign Affairs.

Gmelch, Sharon (Ed.), *Irish Life*, 1979, O'Brien Press.

Gwynn, Stephen, *Reminiscences of a Literary Man*, 1976, Thomas Nelson & Sons Ltd.

Joyce, James, *Ulysses*, 1952, Bodley Head.

Kee, Robert, *Ireland: A History,* 1980, Weidenfeld & Nicolson.

Kennelly, Brendan, *Moloney Up And At It*, 1984, Mercier Press.

Keynes, Geoffrey (Ed.), *The Poetry and Prose of William Blake*, 1961, Nonesuch Library.

Lawlor, H J (Trans.), *St Bernard of Clairvaux: Life of St Malachy of Armagh*, 1920, London.

Lee, J J, *Ireland 1945-70*, 1979, Gill & Macmillan.

Litton, Frank (Ed.), *Unequal Achievement: The Irish Experience 1957-1982*, 1982, The Institute of Public Administration.

Love is for Life, 1985, The Irish Bishops' Pastoral.

Lydon, J F, *Ireland in the Later Middle Ages*, 1981, Irish Academic Press.

Lydon, J F, *The Lordship of Ireland in the Middle Ages*, 1972, Irish Academic Press.

Lyons, F S L, *Culture and Anarchy in Ireland*, 1982, Oxford University Press.

Lyons, F S L, *Ireland Since the Famine*, 1971, Weidenfeld & Nicolson.

MacManus, Francis, *The Years of the Great Test 1929-39*, 1967, Mercier Press.

MacNiaocaill, Gearóid, *Ireland Before the Vikings*, 1972, Gill & Macmillan.

Moody, T W & Martin, F X (Eds), *The Course of Irish History*, 1967, Mercier Press.

Mould, Daphne Pochin, *The Aran Islands*, 1977, David & Charles.

Murphy, John A, *Ireland in the 20th Century*, 1975, Gill & Macmillan.

O'Connor, Frank, *The Backward Look*, 1967, London.

Otway-Ruthven, A J, *A History of Mediaeval Ireland*, 1967, London.

Synge, John, *Collected Plays*, 1950, Gill & Macmillan.

Webb, G C (Ed.), *Metalogicon*, 1929, Oxford.

A cottage window, painted to look like patchwork, in rural Ireland.

PICTURE CREDITS